George Cukor directing Billie Burke, and John Barrymore in *A Bill of Divorcement*

Cukor & Co.

The Films of George Cukor

and His Collaborators

by Gary Carey

The Museum of Modern Art

New York

Distributed by New York Graphic Society Ltd., Greenwich, Conn.

Trustees of
The Museum of Modern Art

© The Museum of Modern Art, 1971
11 West 53 Street, New York, N.Y. 10019
Library of Congress Catalog Card Number 74-100681
ISBN 0-87070-331-5
Designed by Carl Laanes
Type set by Atlantic Linotype Co., Inc., New York
Printed and bound by Publication Press, Inc., Baltimore

Acknowledgments

I would like to thank the following persons for enabling me to see again various films: Martin Blau and Charlotte Walerstein of Columbia Pictures, William Everson, Harry Gittleson of RKO-Radio Pictures, William S. Kenly of Paramount Pictures Corporation, S. Douglas Patterson of Films Incorporated, David V. Picker of United Artists Corporation, Serena Schreiber while at MGM-TV, and Martha Torge while at Warner Brothers Television.

Particular thanks are given to the staff of the Library & Museum of the Performing Arts, The New York Public Library, who answered questions with unfailing good spirits.

The illustrations in this book were drawn from the Film Stills Archive of The Museum of Modern Art except for the stills from *Sylvia Scarlett* and *Holiday*, lent by the Springer/Bettmann Film Archive. The passage from *Holiday* is quoted by permission of Samuel French, Inc.

A series of unpublished interviews which Robert Hughes had with Cukor early in 1967 was of inestimable value. All uncredited quotes by Cukor come from interviews the author had with the director in New York in September 1969.

I would especially like to thank my wife Carol for seeing all the movies with me, reading the text as it developed, and for preparing the final manuscript.

—Gary Carey

Contents

Cukor directing Aldo Ray and Judy Holliday in *The Marrying Kind*

Introduction

The theater is the keynote of Cukor's films. More than any other American motion picture director he has adapted theatrical values to film. His virtues are those generally attributed to the stage rather than to the screen director. Cukor regards the text as inviolate. He has said:

When you do a play or a novel, you should try to know why you are doing it; what is the strength of this thing; what is its point of view? Very often I do the weaknesses of it as well as the strengths. . . . If you slick this up, if you smooth it out—that used to be a tendency in pictures —you rob the thing of its vitality and the reason for doing it. . . .[1]

Cukor's allegiance is to the text, first and foremost, and then to the actor, helping him to develop a characterization that fits with the script's over-all tone.

Cukor's reputation rests justifiably upon his adaptations of plays and novels. Of his forty-eight films, thirty-four come from plays or novels, and over a quarter of his films have as leading characters actors or actresses.[2] Taking this as a clue, some critics have attempted to prove that Cukor's major theme has been theater versus reality, and by pushing and pulling a little, they have extended this to mean illusion versus reality. If this were true, then Cukor's best films should be *A Double Life* and *Les Girls*, which deal directly with this theme. Unfortunately, they are only fair-to-middling. The most one can conclude about Cukor's predilection for backstage stories is that he, like most theater people, relishes shoptalk.

As graceful and adept as his staging generally is, Cukor's personality in film is subservient to that of his writers and actors, and his sensibility can best be grasped from the type of collaborators with whom he worked most felicitously. For this reason, I have called this book *Cukor & Co.* because it is as much a story of his co-workers as it is of the director himself.

The Cukor Playbill

Prior to 1920, the American theater was dominated by the great legendary actors who also acted as producers and directors. These stars appeared occasionally in the classics but mainly in tailor-made vehicles. This is the kind of theater with which Cukor, born in New York in 1899, grew up. His conversation today is still peppered with anecdotes about those fabulous, beplumed and be-draped goddesses—Mrs. Fiske, Alla Nazimova, Sarah Bernhardt, Elsie Ferguson, Yvette Guilbert, Isadora Dun-can—who trod the boards as he watched from out front. The extraordinary empathy and regard Cukor has shown for the actor throughout his career was undoubtedly born at this time.

But the period of star domination was drawing to a close as Cukor entered the theater professionally in 1919 as stage manager of the Chicago company of *The Better 'Ole*. About 1920 the American playwright came of age. For the first time, he gained an importance that could contend with that of the star. Hand in hand came a shift of focus from the star performer to the ensemble, for playwrights no longer wrote to satisfy the ego of one particular actor.

From this shift was born the need for the director. When Cukor announced to his family (of which the other male members were destined to be lawyers) that he was going on the stage, they asked him in perplexity what he intended to do. Cukor answered, without a moment's thought, that he was going to be a director, though he confesses that he really didn't know what a director did. This is not surprising. If one looks through the playbills for this pre-1920 period, there is often no directorial credit, and when there is the credit generally reads "staged by" rather than "directed by." At this time, the function that was to grow into that of the director seems to have been little more than that of a glorified stage manager.

In the twenties, since authors were no longer writing vehicles for stars but plays for actors, the role of the director grew in importance. He became a mediator, sensitive both to the author's script and to the actor's craft. The function of the stage director at this time, and a function that Cukor adapted to his film work, was interpretative rather than creative.

After his apprenticeship as a stage manager, Cukor became resident director of the Lyceum Stock Company in Rochester, New York, in 1920. Undoubtedly this experience strengthened his no-nonsense approach to work and his acceptance of the script as inviolate. Working in stock is strictly a business affair. A play has to be put on with minimum rehearsal time. Under the pressure nerves fray, and the person in charge has to be a cool, diplomatic taskmaster. There is no time for temperament. The director has to depend upon the merits of the script he has chosen to see him through, since there is no time for alterations or for dreaming up fancy touches to hide the play's weaknesses.

In 1925, Cukor was invited by Charles Frohman to join his production company in New York. The first play that Cukor directed was *Antonia*, a Hungarian play by Melchior Lengyl, adapted by Arthur Richman. His second play in New York was a more distinguished effort, a dramatization by Owen Davis of F. Scott Fitzgerald's novel *The Great Gatsby*. Cukor remembers this production fondly as being an intelligent adaptation of the novel.

His next assignment, *Her Cardboard Lover*, a French comedy by Jacques Deval, gave Cukor the chance to direct one of his idols, Laurette Taylor. Departing from her stage image forged by the sweet young thing she had played triumphantly in *Peg o' My Heart* and the other roles written by her husband, J. Hartley Manners, Miss Taylor was to play Simone Massoubre, a lady who smokes, drinks, and is given to appearing in public in her step-ins. Most of Miss Taylor's friends and advisors considered the play to be a cheap bedroom farce, beneath the talents of the actress. However, according to her daughter Marguerite Courtney, Miss Taylor said:

It is the most subtle comedy, and Leslie (Howard) and I will play it like a couple of children.[3]

Nonetheless, it was not easy. Cukor remembers:

She had reached the age where undressing on stage inevitably took artistic toll. She knew it perfectly well, and she had to fight hard to overcome the knowledge. Besides this she was essentially a modest woman. Her strict training, Catholic upbringing—all this made it a very difficult task for her.[4]

The play opened on the road. It played Washington, Baltimore, and Atlantic City, and at each stop the critics agreed with Miss Taylor's friends—they were shocked at Peg o' My Heart playing a doxie. Cukor demurred:

Rarely have I seen such a performance! Simone was a passionate, foolish, neurotic woman and was realized by Laurette with extraordinary subtleness and absolute command. She was comic, distraught, light as a feather and heartbreaking, all at the same time.[5]

The management was nervous about the critical response, and the play closed out of town "for revisions." The play finally opened on Broadway on March 21, 1927, with Jeanne Eagels in the role, and the direction credited to Gilbert Miller.

During the 1926–27 season, Cukor stage managed W. Somerset Maugham's *The Constant Wife*, starring Ethel Barrymore, directed by Gilbert Miller. Cukor's only directorial work this season was a flop, *The Dark*, by Martin Brown, with Louis Calhern and Ann Andrews.

Cukor's next two stage productions in the 1927–28 season both found their way to the screen in the sound period, though under different directors. On December 6, 1927, *Trigger* opened, a play by Lulu Vollmer which concerns a young Southern girl who gains a reputation as a faith healer. As a film it was called *Spitfire*, was directed by John Cromwell, and starred Katharine Hepburn in the part played on stage by Claiborne Foster. About a month later, *A Free Soul*, a play by Willard Mack, adapted from a story by Adela Rogers St. John, opened under Cukor's direction. This was filmed in 1931 under the original title and in 1953 as *The Girl Who Had Everything.*

In 1928 Cukor again had the chance to direct Laurette Taylor, this time in a play written by Zoë Akins. *The Furies*, as it finally opened on March 7, 1928, was a rather conventional play dealing with murder and adultery, but according to Marguerite Courtney:

Zoë Akins had written The Furies *for [Miss Taylor]. Originally it was conceived in terms of music which was to be integrated with the action and the dialogue, but somewhere along the line this concept had been lost and the music dispensed with. Shorn of the music, the play's hybrid nature became manifest, but it had its arresting moments. . . .*[6]

Some critics concurred. Alexander Woollcott, writing for the *New York World*, was fascinated with the play's "curious and inverted beauty" and added that it was "an evening to which the returning Laurette Taylor brought a sensitive, honest, and beautiful performance that was touched with a loveliness of which the secret will die with her." Nonetheless, it did not achieve a long run.

Cukor's experience with Miss Taylor could not have been easy during this production, for it was during this period that the rumors began that she drank. Miss Courtney remarks that one of the comforts for her mother during this production was Cukor's presence:

George Cukor was again directing. He knew her vanity,

capriciousness, her high and mighty airs covering the pitfalls of her ignorance and insecurities, and that once in the harness these things dropped from her as though they never existed.[7]

With this production, Cukor's professional alliance with Miss Taylor ended, though several times he tried to arrange for her to resume her film career. Cukor has said of the actress:

Her face was made for the screen. Laurette was unique; she was a marvelous picture personality (she made several silent films), and a marvelous stage personality. She had eyes that were set far apart, and the light came into her eyes. Her acting on stage was very loose and unconventional.[8]

Miss Taylor was offered the part of Marmee in *Little Women* and later a role in a projected film version of John van Druten's *The Distaff Side* which Cukor was to direct but which failed to come off. Cukor was never to direct Miss Taylor in films.

Probably the best play Cukor directed was his last, *Gypsy* by Maxwell Anderson, which starred Claiborne Foster and Louis Calhern.[9] It concerns a heroine who attempts to lead her life according to her inner direction rather than by the niceties demanded by society. She fails.

Gypsy isn't really a very good play, read now, but it indicates the kind of play that was developing during the twenties. It is neither quite comedy nor drama. An American comedy of manners was being created, highly critical of society but with an optimism that allowed an eventual happy outcome. *Gypsy* was written with two endings, both of which were performed; one was happy, the other had the girl commit suicide. The happy one is more consistent with the general tone of the play.

Of all the plays which he directed on the stage, *Gypsy* is the one which most fully coincides with Cukor's strong points as a film director. His greatest rapport is with comic material that has a strong undercurrent of humanity; he is not at his best with farce or with situation comedy. His particular brand of comedy developed in the Broadway theater in the 1920s. It stems from the English comedy of manners, but it is considerably less artificial than its source, for it undertakes the discussion of contemporary problems with some intensity. Still, it retains the setting of the drawing room or the atelier and the polished, epigrammatic dialogue. *Gypsy* was certainly too light to be considered drama but a little too serious to be considered comedy. It is the kind of play that, for lack of a better term, theatrical encyclopedias refer to as the "serious play."

The "serious play" flourished during the 1920s through the efforts of playwrights such as Jesse Lynch Williams, Rachel Crothers, Philip Barry, S. N. Behrman, and Robert E. Sherwood. Maxwell Anderson (until he discovered he was a poet) also practiced the form. It was a relatively new kind of play during Cukor's apprenticeship in the theater, and it influenced his taste, just as did the balance between the actor and the playwright which was being developed at the same time.

Kay Francis on the set of *Virtuous Sin*

Three Co-Directed Films

By 1929 Cukor had made a small but very reputable name on Broadway. This was the year that marked the successful revolution of the talking motion picture. Anyone with the hint of a stage background was in demand in Hollywood. Cukor joined the exodus to the West Coast. He was dialogue director on Paramount's *River of Romance* before his first major assignment as dialogue director for Lewis Milestone's *All Quiet on the Western Front*, in which he worked closely with the young Lew Ayres.

It was common practice during the early sound period for producers to assign two directors to the same film. One, experienced in silent films, was expected to handle the technical end of things; the other, usually with stage experience, was to handle the actors and dialogue. Cukor filled the latter function on his first three films. All were adaptations of stage plays.

Grumpy (1930). Produced by Paramount Pictures. Co-directed by Cyril Gardner. Script by Doris Anderson, adapted from a play by Horace Hodges and Thomas Wigney Percyval. Photographed by David Abel. With Cyril Maude, Phillips Holmes, Paul Cavanagh, Frances Dade, Halliwell Hobbes.

Grumpy was a successful stage vehicle for English actor-manager Cyril Maude, who was a popular favorite on both sides of the Atlantic. Maude specialized in playing old men, and when *Grumpy* was first produced at Wallack's Theatre in New York in 1913, he was 52 years old; by the time he made the film version he was closer to the age of the character, described in the text of the play as "a very fussy old gentlemen . . . storming at everybody one moment, all heart the next." The play, which is a comedy-mystery involving a jewel theft, was first filmed in 1923 by William deMille. Cukor's film stirred little comment at the time of its release.[10]

Virtuous Sin (1930). Produced by Paramount Pictures. Co-directed by Louis Gasnier. Script by Martin Brown, adapted from Louise Long's translation of the play *The General* by Lajos Zihaly. Photographed by David Abel. Edited by Otho Lovering. With Walter Huston, Kay Francis, Kenneth MacKenna, Paul Cavanagh.

Cukor remembers this film as being an adaptation of a "perfectly dreadful" Hungarian play. The story is set in 1917 Russia, and the heroine must sacrifice her honor to save her husband's life. A note in the Film Study Center of The Museum of Modern Art comments "This was not often done in films of that period." Such material is hopeless unless one is Josef von Sternberg, who thrived on it. Cukor, however, is the antithesis of von Sternberg, and the film is played at face value.

The Royal Family of Broadway (1930). Produced by Paramount Pictures. Co-directed by Cyril Gardner. Script by Herman J. Mankiewicz and Gertrude Purcell, from the play by George S. Kaufman and Edna Ferber. Photographed by George Folsey. Edited by Edward Dmytryk. With Fredric March (Anthony Cavendish), Ina Claire (Julia Cavendish), Mary Brian (Gwen), Charles Starrett (Perry Stewart), Henrietta Crosman (Fanny Cavendish), Frank Conroy (Gilmore Marshall).

Of these three films, *The Royal Family* is by far the best, mainly because of Fredric March's extravagant performance of the narcissistic character of Anthony Cavendish. This part was created on Broadway by Otto Kruger; March played the part in the road company and was seen in Los Angeles where he was cast for the role. *The Royal Family* (the additional words of the film title were added so that people would not think this was a story that concerned the British monarchy) was a Kaufman-Ferber comedy success of the 1927 season, which under light disguise burlesqued the Barrymore-Drew clan, renamed Cavendish. Gertrude Purcell and Herman Mankiewicz, who adapted the script, trimmed most of two trying subplots; consequently the tone of the film is much lighter than that of the play.

Ina Claire, who plays Julia Cavendish, was one of the most delightful stage comediennes from the 1910s to the mid-1940s, but she never attained much success on the screen. The reason for this is not because of an inability to respond to the demands of the new medium, nor even because she never received the best parts. Rather it is because her personality did not come through on film.

Without the flamboyance Fredric March brings to the role of Tony Cavendish, *The Royal Family* would probably be a forgettable film. To re-create a stage role for film, the actor must find the original impetus for the role under radically different conditions and, as is the case here, with different collaborators. March managed to do so, and his performance imparts that particular relish with which theater people dote on theater gossip.

The Royal Family is a film that is in places technically awkward, but in embryo it presents the approach to adaptations of stage plays that Cukor would perfect later. The director must translate the stage picture into film terms, and to do so, he must be extremely sympathetic to the original text. The eye of the theater spectator has much more freedom than the eye of a member of a film audience, which is limited to what the film director wants it to see. The film director must focus for the audience—looking at one actor or two or at the whole spectrum of the action. When the film director has made the wrong decision, the flow is broken. Though it isn't done with any great sophistication, as early as *The Royal Family* Cukor seemed aware of the function of the director as audience. He was to perfect this skill in his later films.

Girls About Town: Kay Francis, Lilyan Tashman

Solo Direction at Paramount

Tarnished Lady (1931). Produced by Paramount Pictures. Script by Donald Ogden Stewart, from his story "New York Lady." Photographed by Larry Williams. Edited by Barney Rogan. With Tallulah Bankhead (Nancy Courtney), Clive Brook (Norman Cravath), Phoebe Foster (Germaine), Alexander Kirkland (Dewitt Taylor), Osgood Perkins (Ben Sterner), Elizabeth Patterson (Mrs. Courtney).

Tarnished Lady marked Cukor's first solo directorial effort and the debut of Tallulah Bankhead in talking films after a great success on the London stage. The critics were favorable to Miss Bankhead but felt that she needed stronger material to do her justice. Unfortunately *Tarnished Lady* was as good a film vehicle as Miss Bankhead was to get in the thirties; she had to wait until 1944, when she starred in *Lifeboat*, directed by Alfred Hitchcock, to show her abilities.

Although Miss Bankhead continued to receive sympathetic reviews from film critics during the thirties, she was never a popular success and not entirely because of indifferent vehicles. In a sense, she is like the young Katharine Hepburn; she comes on strong; she confronts the audience as sheer personality, take it or leave it. But she lacks the soft, winning quality that Hepburn hesitantly reveals when one has had just about enough of such aggressiveness.

Tallulah was of those stage personalities on whom the camera cast a cold eye. The lens did not reveal her delicate beauty, and it made her eyes strangely opaque. Her stance, like her bosom, was saggy. Her voice was the bourbon tenor of a truck driver combined with the broad A's of an English lady. She had a curiously ironic way of playing that was perhaps too *recherché* for the average film audience. She was a curiosity, a *monstre sacré*, too rich for most people's blood.

The scenarist of *Tarnished Lady,* Donald Ogden Stewart, became one of Cukor's frequent collaborators. In all, Stewart's name would appear on the credits of seven Cukor films, notably *Holiday* and *The Philadelphia Story* (Stewart was a disciple of Philip Barry, and his charming 1930 play *Rebound,* which was filmed in 1931, is heavily influenced by Barry). Stewart was also a stage actor (he was in the original companies of *Holiday* and *Rebound*) and a comic novelist and essayist in the style of Robert Benchley, but his humor is often wilder, almost surrealistic. In his first years in Hollywood he was often in charge of the dialogue portions of scripts. His lines for *Tarnished Lady* are quite smart and a good deal sharper than the action of the film.

Tarnished Lady firmly belongs in the woman's picture genre that its title and subtitle, *A Story of a New York Lady,* promise. By far the best sequence in the film is the first. We are introduced to socialite Nancy Courtney as she stands blindfolded, smoking a cigarette. She is choosing the mildest for an advertising endorsement. Here and in a few of the following scenes there is a stylish, light tone that is gradually lost in both script and direction. All that remains to hold interest are the silky, elegant production and the thrust of Miss Bankhead's extraordinary personality.

Women's pictures are by nature lugubrious, and Cukor does not stint. Certainly the scene in which Nancy invites her lover for one night of bliss among the sand dunes of Long Island, with gypsy music in the background, might well represent all that is awful in the genre.

Girls About Town (1931). Produced by Paramount Pictures. Story by Zoë Akins. Script by Raymond Griffith and Brian Marlow. Photographed by Ernest Haller. With Kay Francis (Wanda Howard), Joel McCrea (Jim

Tarnished Lady: Tallulah Bankhead, Alexander Kirkland
Girls About Town: Kay Francis, Louise Beavers, Lilyan Tashman

Baker), Lilyan Tashman (Marie Bailey), Eugene Pallette (Benjamin Thomas), Allan Dinehart (Jerry Chase), Lucile Gleason (Mrs. Thomas).

Variety commented in its review of this film, "Maybe Par shoved this out to beat UA's *Greeks Had a Word for It* to the market post." *The Greeks Had a Word for It* and the original story for *Girls About Town* were both written by Zoë Akins and both involve gold diggers. Miss Akins, whose play, *The Furies*, had been directed by Cukor, would write four scripts for him, *Camille, Girls About Town, Zaza,* and *Desire Me*. Miss Akins began working in films in 1930, and she was a specialist in the woman's film. As absurd as these films seem today, within the context of their time they were an impassioned portrayal of the emancipated woman.

Though *Girls About Town* has a top-heavy main story (further weighed down by the insipid playing of Joel McCrea and Kay Francis), the minor characters keep the film bubbly and snappy. Lilyan Tashman is perfectly delightful as Miss Francis' sidekick; she is one of those breezy, wisecracking blondes that thirties films spawned so prodigiously. Whenever she or Eugene Pallette or Lucile Gleason are on screen the film perks up considerably.

The film opens with a razzle-dazzle montage of the girls' café-society existence which, though clichéd, is very smoothly edited and bouncy in its over-all effect. (There are many such montages in Cukor's early films, but I doubt that he had much to do with either their creation or execution.) He gives the McCrea-Francis scenes their full worth, which is nil, but makes the most of the comedy scenes. The scene in which the two girls, in order to raise some quick cash, auction off their clothes, furs, and other belongings to their gold-digging friends is the first of the many scenes or entire films in which Cukor proves his adeptness at handling the many facets of femininity.

One Hour with You (1932). Produced by Ernst Lubitsch for Paramount Pictures. Directed by Lubitsch and Cukor. Script by Samson Raphaelson, from an operetta by Lother Goldschmidt. Photographed by Victor Milner. Music by Richard Whiting. Lyrics by Leo Robin. With Maurice Chevalier (Dr. André Berthier), Jeanette MacDonald (Colette Berthier), Genevieve Tobin (Mitzi), Charles Ruggles (Professor Olivier).

There is some dispute about how great a role Cukor played in the production of *One Hour with You*. He has contradicted himself in two interviews, one time saying he had relatively little to do with it, another time saying he, in effect, directed the entire film. If he did, it must have been from a shooting script very carefully planned by Lubitsch. *One Hour with You* is a charming film; it is a crowning jewel in Lubitsch's career, but of only marginal importance in Cukor's. Scriptwriter, photographer, actors, composer, and lyricist were all favored confreres of Lubitsch. The film, a remake of a silent Lubitsch film, *The Marriage Circle*, has music and plot intertwined in a way that is typical of the director. It reflects little of Cukor's personality as found in his own comedies or musicals.

Jean Parker, Katharine Hepburn, and Cukor on the set of
Little Women

The Selznick Years

Cukor has said of the beginning of his relationship with producer David O. Selznick:

I met David Selznick a day or so after I came out to Hollywood. He was a young assistant to a producer, Benny Feinman. He had no office, but he would run around and he was "full of beans." Then we became great, great friends. And then, when he went to RKO, he had a kind of excitement about him, and he sprung me. I was doing rather badly at Paramount; my talent wasn't appreciated. But as is generally the way with people—Paramount didn't want me until someone else did; the whole thing became really complicated. But Selznick arranged for me to go to RKO and work with their biggest star at the time, Connie Bennett. It was rather early in the game. From then on Selznick and I worked together on a great many pictures. I think we had a salubrious influence on each other. We even withstood for whatever reason my removal from Gone with the Wind—*we remained good friends. We never worked together again, but he was always planning things, and I would like to have worked with him again. I know that working with him had an effect on me, and I should think I had an effect on him. He had enthusiasm. He had a kind of gusto, and he would take a chance, and it was enormous fun to work with him. He was a real showman.*[11]

In addition to the single film he made for Paramount, Cukor made three films in 1932 for RKO. From this we can gather that the films had short shooting schedules. With the exception of *A Bill of Divorcement*, Cukor's first films for RKO were not prestigious productions; in fact, *Rockabye* was clearly just an excuse to keep Constance Bennett before her public. But because they were done swiftly and because RKO did not have the resources for elaborate productions, they remain modest "quickies" and are modestly enjoyable.

What Price Hollywood (1932). Produced by David O. Selznick for RKO Radio Pictures. Script by Jane Murfin and Ben Markson, from an adaptation by Gene Fowler and Rowland Brown of a story by Adela Rogers St. John. Photographed by Charles Rosher. Edited by Jack Kitchin. With Constance Bennett (Mary Evans), Lowell Sherman (Max Carey), Neil Hamilton (Lenny Borden), Gregory Ratoff (Julius Saxe), Louise Beavers (Cassie), Eddie Anderson (James).

David O. Selznick has said that his later production, *A Star Is Born,* was inspired by and fashioned from *What Price Hollywood.*[12] The story lines of these films are remarkably similar. In *What Price Hollywood,* a waitress at the Brown Derby restaurant meets an alcoholic director who gives her a break in film. Her career ascends while his descends. The story of *A Star Is Born* is exactly the same in outline, substituting an actress for the waitress and a drunken actor for the alcoholic director. *A Star Is Born* also contains a number of scenes that are very reminiscent of *What Price Hollywood:* in one film the actress is mobbed by her fans on her wedding day; in the other, she is besieged at her husband's funeral. The true *auteurist* will delight in a number of touches that recur in Cukor's version of *A Star Is Born;* for example in each film, as the actress puts on her make-up for her screen test, her face is reflected in three mirrors.

I think that we can assume that since Selznick felt that it was necessary to refashion *What Price Hollywood* four years later (the first version of *A Star Is Born* appeared in 1936), he must have regarded the earlier film as only a trial balloon. Certainly there was more to this subject than was achieved at first try. The script of *What Price Hollywood* isn't very well constructed. Halfway through it is sidetracked by an extraneous romance and marriage of the actress. For this film to be the trenchant study of

What Price Hollywood: Constance Bennett, Lowell Sherman

Hollywood which it seems to intend, the central relationship between the actress and her director needs not only greater emphasis but also greater depth.

Lowell Sherman may have patterned his role on his brother-in-law, John Barrymore, who was also a friend of Cukor and screenwriter Gene Fowler, who later wrote Barrymore's biography, *Good Night, Sweet Prince*. Sherman brings to the early section of the film that light self-mockery with which Barrymore frequently guyed the ineptitudes of his late comedy roles. In the drunk scenes, Sherman retains an air of refinement and sensitivity. He plays totally without self-pity and without asking for sympathy, even in his suicide scenes. It is the first of a number of drunk scenes in Cukor's films, and in them all (particularly in *A Star Is Born* and *Holiday*) the director shows a remarkable sympathy but no bathos toward the problem of alcoholism.

The film has its vulgarities, particularly a moment when Sherman pulls a fully dressed Louise Beavers into a swimming pool with him. The scenes concerning Miss Beavers and Eddie Anderson are guaranteed to irritate those who find Hollywood Negro humor of this period offensive. Otherwise the direction is silken smooth, nicely balancing the comic and serious moments. Interestingly enough, some of the Neil Hamilton-Constance Bennett scenes here (and a conple of the Joel McCrea-Constance Bennett scenes in *Rockabye*) have the same roustabout romantics as did the screwball comedies, a genre that Cukor otherwise never tried.

Cukor's second film for Selznick was a film adaptation of *A Bill of Divorcement*, a play that had been a great stage success in 1921. Clemence Dane had written the play at a time when a bill, intended to liberalize existing English divorce laws, was under discussion. The play, which is a plea for adopting this bill, assumes that its new amendments have already become law. The play concerns a man still suffering from the effects of shell shock. His wife has divorced him and is planning to marry another man, when the husband suddenly recovers. The wife, torn between love and pity, has almost decided to remain dutifully with her former husband, when their daughter, renouncing her own fiancé, takes the care of her father upon herself. The daughter's martyrdom is motivated by her belief that there is a taint of insanity on her father's side of the family that, if she marries, may be passed on to her children. This suspicion, however, is only an unsubstantiated rumor, so that the daughter's act seems less noble than foolish. By the time the film was made, the divorce bill had been passed and was a dead issue. Without this timeliness, the contrived plot and hollow characters are ruthlessly exposed. The play is also monumentally talky, and the talk is a low grade of high seriousness, for example, "I'm withering without you like cut grass in the sun."

A Bill of Divorcement (1932). Produced by David O. Selznick for RKO Radio Pictures. Screenplay by Howard Estabrook and Harry Wagstaff Gribble, based on the play by Clemence Dane. Photographed by Sid Hickox. Edited by Arthur Roberts. With John Barrymore (Hilary Fairchild), Katharine Hepburn (Sydney Fairchild), Billie Burke (Margaret Fairchild), David Manners (Kit), Paul Cavanagh (Gray), Bramwell Fletcher (Gareth), Henry Stephenson (Dr. Alliott), Elizabeth Patterson (Aunt Hester).

Cukor has said of his approach to this film:
What dictates your approach very often isn't you, but it's the situation—it's the text. It's what the play tells you. I envy directors who have everything written on a piece of paper and then just go up on set and do it. I can't make

up dialogue, but I see things. The actors suggest things to me. . . . Some people are in themselves fascinating, you get them in a strong situation, and you do it simply, and it carries you along with it. Well, Barrymore was that kind of person, and the situation in Bill *of Divorcement was very strong. You just "ride it." You do it naturally, I suppose. Something—a clock or something goes off in your head and you think, "That's the way to do it." Sometimes you're not right; sometimes you're too slow. But if it's a good strong situation—and you have interesting people who carry it, and you're in the saddle. . . .*[13]

Cukor was a great admirer of Barrymore's acting, and he was enthralled by working with him. Cukor responded to the actor's greatness but failed to see that the greatness exposed the two-dimensionality of the role. Barrymore, a fine actor in the heroic mold, was simply too large for the meager part of Hilary. With all the resources at his command, Barrymore attempted to make the role soar, but it stubbornly remained earthbound.

For the part of Sydney, Cukor chose Katharine Hepburn, a stage actress whose reputation was based mainly on being fired from a number of plays. In 1932, however, she had scored a success on the stage in *The Warrior's Husband.* Cukor admits that he is not sure why he chose Hepburn to play the part since her screen test (a scene from Philip Barry's *Holiday*) was mediocre. "At the end," he recalls, "she placed a glass on the floor and something about the gesture was very, very moving. She was like no one I had ever seen." He continues by saying that during the first few days of shooting he still didn't know what to make of her.

The record shows that Hepburn had an electrifying effect on the public. Certainly there is an arresting personality at work here, but the personality hasn't come to terms with the demands of the camera. There is still

A Bill of Divorcement: Katharine Hepburn, John Barrymore
Rockabye: Paul Lukas, Constance Bennett

the scent of the theater about her performance. Hepburn seems gawky, and yet there are moments which are touched with the most casual gracefulness. There is a vividness about her that draws us and makes us want to see more.

Rockabye (1932). Produced by David O. Selznick for RKO Radio Pictures. Script by Jane Murfin and Kubec Glasmon, from a play by Lucia Bronder. Photographed by Charles Rosher. Edited by George Hively. With Constance Bennett (Judy), Joel McCrea (Jake Pell), Paul Lukas (De Sola), Jobyna Howland (Snooks), Walter Pidgeon (Commissioner Howard), Walter Catlett (Dunn), Virginia Hammond (Mrs. Pell), J. M. Kerrigan (Dugan), June Filmer (Lilly Bet), Sterling Holloway (Man in Night Club).

There is an inside joke in *What Price Hollywood*, when Miss Bennett, playing an actress, asks if she must have a baby in every film. Miss Bennett always did, sometimes out of wedlock, sometimes legitimized just within the last of the nine months. *Rockabye* concerns a glamorous stage star's attempt to play motherhood, and there is some ambiguity in the script as to whether the baby is adopted or her own illegitimate child.

The emptiness of the script invites any kind of falderal to keep it alive; the actress, mentioning she loves balloons, finds her bedroom filled with balloons by the man she loves. As Miss Bennett leaves her boudoir, kicking the balloons, photographed in creamy tones, the plastic values of the *mise en scène* justify the segment and provide the high point of the film.

As for the rest, it's standard stuff. Cukor seems to have let everyone have his head. Constance Bennett chews up the scenery, and in one song number (this is the period in which leading ladies always had a song number), she carries on with gestures that defy description. Even worse is Jobyna Howland as the actress's alcoholic mother who tries to steal each scene in which she appears and fails every time.

Our Betters (1933). Produced by David O. Selznick for RKO Radio Pictures. Script by Jane Murfin and Harry Wagstaff Gribble, from the play by W. Somerset Maugham. Photographed by Charles Roscher and James Kitchin. With Constance Bennett (Lady Pearl Grayston), Gilbert Roland (Pepi D'Costa), Charles Starrett (Fleming Harvey), Anita Louise (Bessie), Grant Mitchell (Thorton Clay), Hugh Sinclair (Lord Beane), Alan Mowbray (Lord George Grayston), Minor Watson (Arthur Fenwick), Violet Kemble-Cooper (Duchess), Tyrell Davis (Ernest).

Our Betters is Cukor's only attempt at bringing English high comedy to the screen. This is a form of theater that has never been very successfully handled by American actors who are not trained in vocal nuance and that tradition of theater in which the frivolous is taken with utter seriousness.

Maugham's play is a little darker than most high comedies—it is an often bitter exposé of expatriate American women who have married Englishmen for their titles—but still it is high comedy, and Cukor wasn't able to assemble a company equal to the demands of the form. Only Violet Kemble-Cooper, as the Duchess, has the technique and manner. Constance Bennett in the leading role (a part that Ina Claire played with great success on the stage) is properly soignée; her gowns have been designed to make the most of entrances and exits; she strikes poses out of *Vanity Fair.* Perhaps out of desperation Cukor gave her a mile-long cigarette holder, and, out of desperation, Miss Bennett molds her performance around it.

Maugham shows the women of the play as catty, frivolous, adulterous, and vulgar social climbers. There is a testiness in the writing (though the film script and Cukor's direction tend to soften it) which casts more suspicion on Maugham's attitude toward femininity in general than on these women in particular. Though much better constructed and a great deal wittier, *Our Betters* is uncomfortably close to Clare Booth's *The Women*, and Cukor's films of these plays I find disagreeable.

David O. Selznick's record at RKO was so outstanding that he was offered a job at MGM by his father-in-law, Louis B. Mayer. Part of Selznick's reason for accepting was the fact that the new head of RKO, Merlin Hall Aylesworth, insisted on having final approval on everything concerned with production. Selznick's first production at MGM was *Dinner at Eight*, and to direct it he brought Cukor with him from RKO.

Dinner at Eight (1933). Produced by David O. Selznick for Metro-Goldwyn-Mayer. Script by Herman Mankiewicz and Frances Marion from the play by George S. Kaufman and Edna Ferber. Additional dialogue by Donald Ogden Stewart. Photographed by William Daniels. Edited by Ben Lewis. With Marie Dressler (Carlotta Vance), John Barrymore (Larry Renault), Wallace Beery (Dan Packard), Jean Harlow (Kitty Packard), Lionel Barrymore (Oliver Jordan), Lee Tracy (Max Kane), Edmund Lowe (Dr. Wayne Talbot), Billie Burke (Millicent Jordan), Madge Evans (Paula Jordan), Jean Hersholt (Jo Stengel), Karen Morley (Mrs. Wayne Talbot), Louise Closser Hale (Hattie Loomis), Phillips Holmes (Ernest de Graff), May Robson (Mrs. Wendel), Grant Mitchell (Ed Loomis), Phoebe Foster (Miss Alden), Elizabeth Patterson (Miss Copeland).

Our Betters: Alan Mowbray, Constance Bennett
Dinner at Eight: Jean Harlow

Certain rare plays, such as *Dinner at Eight*, seem destined for the movies. When it opened on Broadway, it was considered highly cinematic because of the great number of elaborate scene changes required. Though this does make it ideally suitable for the medium, there is a more cogent reason to explain why the film version of *Dinner at Eight* is so much better than any stage production could hope to be. It offered a large number of roles begging to be filled by star personalities. *Dinner at Eight* demands larger-than-life personalities, and MGM, boasting of "more stars than there are in heaven," was the ideal company to undertake this project as it had the year before with *Grand Hotel* and would later with *The Women.*

Dinner at Eight, despite the fact that it was a roaring success on stage, never could have been a very good play. It is an extremely thin piece of writing and has a number of lifeless scenes. The film script has been brightened up, the dialogue has been sharpened a bit, and a relatively happy ending has been supplied. (The happy ending, incidentally, is a great improvement; for certain material, "honest" unhappy endings are really dishonest.) There is also a slight shift of emphasis among the roles, partly owing to the impact of the players, partly owing to changes in the script. Marie Dressler's Carlotta Vance probably is somewhat bawdier than Kaufman and Ferber had imagined the character (the part was played by Constance Collier on the stage), but she is just as beguiling. The script was co-written by Frances Marion, a Hollywood pro who wrote many of the Mary Pickford films in the silent period and in the talkie period specialized in material for Miss Dressler. The famous final exchange of dialogue between Miss Dressler and Jean Harlow is entirely the creation of the Hollywood writers.

Equally felicitous is the casting of Jean Harlow and Wallace Beery as the *nouveau riche* Packards; it is virtually impossible to imagine anyone else playing these roles (when the play was revived by Tyrone Guthrie in 1967, the memory of the film strangled the production like a resentful ghost). Harlow's strident, hard-as-nails cheapness is beautifully offset by Adrian's sleek white gowns. This symphony in white shrieks like a banshee, and Beery is her match at pacing insults. Their scenes together are masterpieces of making the disagreeable comic.

Harlow, Dressler, and Beery make the film the great, good fun that it is. Nothing much is done to improve the dreary melodramatic plots involving Edmund Lowe as the doctor with too much of a bedside manner and John Barrymore as a has-been, alcoholic actor. I don't think that there can be much doubt that Ferber and Kaufman, who had previously used Barrymore as the model for Tony Cavendish in *The Royal Family*, had Barrymore in mind when they wrote the role of Larry Renault. It's a little embarrassing seeing an actor playing a character based so unflatteringly on his own life. Barrymore was not, at this point, a has-been, as is Larry Renault, but his reputation was already suffering from a disappointing film career and increasing alcoholic misconduct. Later in his career, when, for instance, he found himself playing with Mary Beth Hughes in *The Great Profile*, he performed with a kind of wide-eyed mockery that put everything, including himself, in perspective. The role of Larry Renault, however, brought out an unpleasing self-pity in the actor.

With the expertise of MGM's technical staff behind him, Cukor gave *Dinner at Eight* the glossiest, costliest look of any of his films to date. Though many of the sequences use multiple camera set-ups and rapid cutting (notice particularly the first scene in the Packard's bedroom), Cukor relies on those long takes (used best in a scene between Marie Dressler and Lionel Barrymore in the latter's office) which became a trademark of his films.

A number of critics complained that Cukor had slackened the pace at which the play was staged on Broadway. This is an accusation that Cukor would face many times during his career, but *Dinner at Eight* is played at a good clip. Film rhythm is conventionally conveyed by editing, and long takes may seem slow. There is, however, another kind of film rhythm, that conveyed by the actor within the shot, and it is this rhythm that Cukor often uses.

Selznick still had one picture to finish on his contract with RKO, so he and Cukor returned to make *Little Women*, adapted from Louisa May Alcott's novel. Whether Selznick actually did much work on the film seems doubtful, since the film's titles credit Merian C. Cooper as Executive Producer and Kenneth Macgowan as Associate Producer.

Alistair Cooke was visiting Hollywood at this period, and he saw Cukor while he was on location at Warner's ranch, where the March and Laurence homes had been built as sets. Mr. Cooke recorded his visit in *The Listener*. Never one to mince words, Mr. Cooke began the interview by lamenting "the current confusion between making films and making photographic records of stage plays." Cukor answered:

I've been in pictures for four years, and still have to stop myself focusing and grouping as I did for the stage. I admit I—and theater directors like me, Mamoulian, for example —would be the first to confess we have a lot to learn. But we have a special function in films like this—adaptations from novels and stage plays—where to know the difficulties of stage presentation is to be readier to see where the camera can overcome them. I grant you that stories written for the screen should be impossible to perform elsewhere. But here, for instance, I'm trying to make a careful visual reproduction of a story that thousands of people know by heart. The temptations are not merely technical ones.

Cooke asked whether Cukor meant that "it might be thought smart to guy *Little Women* in 1933." Cukor responded,

Yes, or take it very solemnly and make it heavy and sentimental. Really, it's charming and unpretentious.[14]

Little Women (1933). Produced by David O. Selznick for RKO Radio Pictures. Screenplay by Sarah Y. Mason and Victor Heerman, from the novel by Louisa May Alcott. Photographed by Henry Gerrard. Edited by Jack Kitchin. With Katharine Hepburn (Jo March), Joan Bennett (Amy March), Frances Dee (Meg March), Jean Parker (Beth March), Spring Byington (Marmee), Edna May Oliver (Aunt March), Douglass Montgomery (Laurie), Henry Stephenson (Mr. Laurence), John Davis Lodge (Brooks), Mable Concord (Hannah), Nydia Westman (Mamie), Samuel Hinds (Mr. March), Paul Lukas (Fritz Bhaer).

Little Women is a very special film. It is openly sentimental, but we don't feel embarrassed at being moved by it. We never laugh at it (as we do at the later, quite terrible 1949 remake), but instead smile with affection and tenderness. George Cukor's re-creation of Louisa May Alcott's world presents us with sentimentality as a style of life, or as a way of seeing the world. It may not do for our world, but we look back with friendliness and some nostalgia to a time when it was possible to live with charm, sweetness, and unguarded emotions.

Not all of *Little Women* is so good. Some of it falls into the trap of the artificial dramatic conventions usual in depicting material that is frankly sentimental. Max Steiner's soupy score underlines each dramatic crisis with the same insistent theme. Quite the worst moment in the film (and one which almost wrecks our immersion in the world Cukor has led us to accept) is when sick Beth (played by Jean Parker) struggles to walk across a room into her father's arms with an ecstasy most befitting Teresa of Avila. I wish Katharine Hepburn as Jo, while listening to *Lieder*, did not lean against the piano quite so artfully with her chin thrust ever so cleverly forward to catch the light; this is not Jo giving herself up to the enjoyment of Schubert, but some movie queen showing that she knows the better things in life when she hears them. But these failings are inconsequential against the total achievement.

This is the first of Cukor's films that leave visual images in one's mind that turn up months, years after one has seen the film. There is Jo, her skirts tucked up around her hoop, making a snowman; the party at Laurie's at which the guests dance waltzes, lancers, and polkas, creating one of the loveliest moments of Americana in all of film. Most persistent of all is Jo sitting on the ground with brilliant diffused sunlight all around her, refusing Laurie's proposal, not wanting to hurt but knowing she must. *Little Women* is the most visually sophisticated of Cukor's films to date. It is beautifully lit and uses a number of imaginative camera placements, but as is typical with Cukor nothing calls attention to itself.

The art direction is excellent. The March and the Laurence homes, which dominate the film, were designed by Herb Erwin, a New York artist and decorator, and they are remarkable examples of delineating characters by background. Both express Victorian Americana at its loveliest. The March home is simple, warm, and comfortable, striking because of its genuineness. The Laurence home, much vaster, is a collector's dream of quaintly ornate and beautiful candelabra, chandeliers, and chairs. The March home glows with the warmth of homely affection; the Laurence house, with the warmth of tasteful wealth.

Throughout the film Cukor re-creates with great sensitivity the exact atmosphere and feeling that Miss Alcott achieves in her novel; see for instance the scene in which the sisters put on a Christmas play, *The Witch's Curse*, that Jo has written for the neighborhood girls. In the book it is described thus:

On Christmas night, a dozen girls piled onto the bed which was the dress circle, and sat before the blue and yellow chintz curtains in a most flattering state of expectancy. There was a great deal of rustling and whispering behind the curtain, a trifle of lamp smoke, and an occasional giggle from Amy, who was apt to get hysterical in the excitement of the moment. Presently a bell sounded, the curtain flew apart, and the Operatic Tragedy began. . . . A good deal of hammering went on before the curtain rose again; but when it became evident what a masterpiece of stage carpentry had been got up, no one muttered at the delay. It was truly superb! A tower rose to the ceiling; halfway up appeared a window, with a lamp burning at it, and behind the white curtain appeared Zara in a lovely blue and silver dress, waiting for Roderigo. He came in gorgeous array, with plumed cap, red cloak, chestnut lovelocks, a guitar and the boots, of course. . . . Then came the grand effect of the play. Roderigo produced a rope ladder, with five steps to it, threw up one end, and invited Zara to descend. Timidly she crept from the lattice, put her hand on Roderigo's shoulder, and was about to leap gracefully down, when "Alas! alas for Zara!" she forgot her train—it caught in the window; the tower tottered, leaned forward, fell with a crash, and buried the unhappy lovers in the ruins.

In practically every detail this passage is re-created on the screen with exactly the same note of mock-serious enjoyment of amateur theatricals. Not surprisingly, Cukor has added a number of loving details to the backstage

activities that are entirely in keeping with the tenor of
the scene. Amy's unwillingness to faint and soil her gown
is a master stroke which Miss Alcott would have ap-
plauded. It is one of the most delicious moments in the
film.

Much of the success of the film comes from the excellent script by Sarah Y. Mason and Victor Heerman.
Wisely, most of the dialogue is taken directly from Miss
Alcott's pen. Though the action has been greatly tele-
scoped, there is never any feeling of abruptness or discon-
tinuity. Also there is a much surer sense of dramatic
contrast here than there is in the novel, as is shown in the
juxtaposition of Jo's refusal of Laurie and Meg's marriage
to Brooks, and in placing Jo's acceptance of Dr. Bhaer's
proposal in the midst of Laurie and Amy's homecoming.

The triumph of the film, however, is really Katharine
Hepburn's Jo. The actress is brilliant, and without her the
film would not be the small miracle it is. Her Jo gives the
film a spine, and not only because the script gives her
character primary importance. Partly it is because this is
inspired casting. Hepburn's own individuality and vibrancy
filters through the character of Jo, so that beneath the
sentimentality comes a steely strength and intelligence.
Though she gives the tender scenes their full due—indeed,
her refusal of Laurie's proposal with its delicately por-
trayed emotion is quite her most sensitive piece of acting
up to this time—it is Hepburn's own strength of character
which makes us accept the validity of many moments of
the film which we might otherwise reject.

After finishing *Little Women*, Cukor returned to MGM to
work on Selznick's production of *David Copperfield*.

David Copperfield (1935). Produced by David O. Selznick for Metro-Goldwyn-Mayer. Screenplay by Howard

Little Women: Katharine Hepburn
David Copperfield: W. C. Fields, Freddie Bartholomew

Estabrook from Hugh Walpole's adaptation of Charles Dickens's novel. Photographed by Oliver T. Marsh. Edited by Robert J. Kern. With W. C. Fields (Mr. Micawber), Lionel Barrymore (Dan Peggotty), Maureen O'Sullivan (Dora Spenlow), Madge Evans (Agnes Wickfield), Edna May Oliver (Aunt Betsy), Lewis Stone (Mr. Wickfield), Freddie Bartholomew (David Copperfield, as a boy), Frank Lawton (David Copperfield, as a young man), Elizabeth Allan (Clara Copperfield), Roland Young (Uriah Heep), Basil Rathbone (Mr. Murdstone), Elsa Lanchester (Clickett), Jean Cadell (Mrs. Micawber), Violet Kemble-Cooper (Jane Murdstone), Una O'Connor (Mrs. Gummidge).

Someone who worked for MGM in the early thirties told me that the company's executives were fond of giving guided tours of the lot for important visitors. The tour would end by showing the visitor Hugh Walpole sitting at his desk, writing the treatment for *David Copperfield* with a long quill pen. Perhaps the story is apocryphal, but it fits perfectly. The film itself has the same blend of reverence and showing off.

The screenplay is a fair adaptation of the novel. What is wrong is the over-all tone of the direction and acting. Most of the supporting players are simply too arch ("Look, duckie, we're playing Dickens!"). On the other hand the juveniles play with an insipidity entirely befitting Dickens.

A few of the actors succeed. Edna May Oliver, Jean Cadell (a great English stage star of the period), and Basil Rathbone, for instance, present workable impressions of the characters in the book. Roland Young gives a good performance as Uriah Heep, though one is perhaps a little too aware of his efforts to turn his own impish charm into Uriah's unctuousness. Freddie Bartholomew's tony voice and general femininity are revolting in a child his age, but still he is genuinely affecting in a number of scenes. He is probably a great deal better than Jackie Cooper, whom Louis B. Mayer wanted for the role.

Also unhappy is the casting of W. C. Fields as Mr. Micawber. Though physically ideal, his personality isn't expansive enough, and the role contracts into a small ball of stinginess and misanthropy. One is aware of a famous comedian hamstrung with a part he has to play. Fields wasn't first choice for the part. Charles Laughton had been cast in the role but withdrew because he feared he wouldn't be sympathetic enough.

The film fails to capture the imagination partly because of the uninspired art direction. Cukor and the MGM art department evidently did a great deal of careful research concerning the design of this film, but even as studio reality, it doesn't convince as did the settings for *Little Women*. It is decorative; perhaps we even "ooh and aah" over individual settings. Somehow the look of Cukor's *David Copperfield* isn't convincing, and nothing else about the film changes this initial response.

Jumping ahead a few years, Cukor's and David Selznick's professional alliance ended ten days after the shooting of **Gone with the Wind** began. It had first been announced that Cukor was to direct the film in October 1936. As soon as he had finished the editing of *Camille*, Cukor began the famous talent search for Scarlett O'Hara, though according to Vivien Leigh, who finally played the role, the director had always wanted Katharine Hepburn for Scarlett.[15]

Shooting began the last week of January 1938 without a completed script. Cukor began with the scene between Scarlett and the Tarleton brothers on the steps of Tara and from there proceeded to shoot more or less chronologically. Shooting stopped while Olivia de Havilland and

Vivien Leigh were rehearsing the Atlanta charity ball scene. The actresses were told that Cukor had been removed from the film. They pleaded with Selznick to have him reinstated but without success.

The reasons behind Selznick's dismissal of Cukor are not known. It has been conjectured that the producer felt that Cukor was spending too much time on intimate detail and ignoring the sweep of the production. Olivia de Havilland has commented:

George Cukor is the Cellini of directors. He has a marvelously intricate imagination which works on a very fine scale. Take a look at the scene where Mammy's lacing up Scarlett—it's just crammed with tiny fleeting expressions and motives—and then at the next one, where Scarlett sits on the stairs eating a chicken leg. There's no other scene in the film with so much detail, such richness—those were Cukor touches.[16]

Nonetheless, Selznick evidently felt these touches were taking up too much time. He told Kenneth Tynan:

Basically, George was a transplanted stage director. He didn't know about cutting. I knew he wouldn't want to be bothered with the spectacular side of the picture, the military stuff.[17]

Another factor in the removal of Cukor from the film was that Clark Gable felt that he was being short-changed by the attention the director was giving the ladies; since Gable was, with the exception of the novel itself, the biggest box-office draw in the film, his wish had to be respected. Victor Fleming, Sidney Franklin, William Wellman, and Sam Wood all directed parts of the film, but Fleming alone received directorial credit.

Although Cukor was off the set, he still had an influence on the film, or so Vivien Leigh claimed:

I'd never have been able to get through without the book and George Cukor. I'd keep the book beside me and look

*up each scene as we filmed it to remind me where I was
supposed to be, and how I should be feeling, until Selznick
shouted at me to throw the damned thing away. On Sun-
days, when we didn't shoot, I'd steal over to George
Cukor's and discuss with him the bits we'd be working on
the next week. It was probably terribly irregular, but I
couldn't have finished it without him.*[18]

Only later did Miss Leigh learn that Olivia de Havilland
was doing the same thing by telephone.

Being removed from a production of this size and
importance could not have been a pleasant experience for
Cukor. Today, however, he is philosophical:

You know, when I was put off Gone with the Wind—
*well, that should have buried me. Well, I never thought
they were right to do it. . . . In my experience, there've
been some people removed from pictures . . . I've called
them several times and said, "Look here, if it's any com-
fort to you, I'm still around and I was put off the biggest
picture ever made. And here I am to tell the tale."*[19]

Sylvia Scarlett:
Dennie Moore, Katharine Hepburn, Edmund Gwenn

Hosenrolle

While Selznick was working elsewhere, Cukor returned
to RKO to make one last film. This film, *Sylvia Scarlett*,
is shrouded in mystery. It was a financial and critical
disaster for reasons that neither the critics nor the partici-
pants seem able to pinpoint. It is rarely revived and sel-
dom shown even on television. It is possible that its
failure prevented Cukor from dealing with more offbeat,
potentially uncommercial material in the future. Yet when
Cukor speaks about it, it is with a nervous affection, and
one has the feeling that it is one of his favorites. Katharine
Hepburn, the star of the film, has spoken of the first
preview of the film:

*We did this picture about which George secretly thought
to himself, "Something is a bit wrong with this," and I
was thinking to myself, "Something is a bit wrong with
this," but we went on. . . . I played the part of a boy
through seven-eighths of the picture. This picture was supposed to be magical and hilarious comedy; it was Teddy
Gwenn's first picture. It was Cary Grant's first decent
part because George knew Cary and cast him as a character comedian, which is what he made his career on. He
was the only thing that really made a hit in* Sylvia Scarlett.
*Well, we took the picture to the preview and it started
and not a sound from the audience. And Natalie Paley,
who was in it, said to me, "Kate, why don't they laugh?"
And I said, "Well, Natalie, they don't think it's funny!"
They didn't know what it was about; they were leaving in
droves; and I got up and went to the ladies room and a
woman was just lying there in a dead faint; and I thought,
"Well, that picture killed her, obviously." Well we went
back to George's place, George and I. There was nothing
to do but laugh. It was a disaster; and it had been quite
expensive for those days, over a million dollars. Pandro
Berman, the producer, met us at George's, and he was
in a total panic. We said, "Pandro, we'll do another pic-*

ture for you—for nothing." Seriously, we said this. Pandro said, "I don't want either of you ever to work for me again."[20]

Both Hepburn and Cukor were to work for Berman again. Cukor however, whether by choice or expulsion, did not work at RKO after this.

Sylvia Scarlett (1936). Produced by Pandro S. Berman for RKO Radio Pictures. Script by Gladys Unger, John Collier, and Mortimer Offner, adapted from a novel by Compton MacKenzie. Photographed by Joseph August. Edited by Jane Loring. With Katharine Hepburn (Sylvia Snow, Sylvia Scarlett, Sylvester Scarlett), Cary Grant (Jimmie Monkley), Brian Aherne (Michael Fane), Edmund Gwenn (Henry Snow, Henry Scarlett), Natalie Paley (Lily), Dennie Moore (Maudie Tilt).

Sylvia Scarlett opens with a written preface: "To the adventurer, all who stray from the beaten track, life is an extravagance in which laughter and luck and love come in odd ways, but they are nonetheless sweet for that." The words suggest a mixture of the worlds of Horatio Alger and James M. Barrie, a Victorian never-never land of whimsy, melodrama, and sentimentality. In the first half of the film, director and cast unabashedly enjoy but never guy the pretense of the world they are creating.

Katharine Hepburn's Sylvia belongs to the world of James M. Barrie, an author to whom she seemingly felt drawn, since she filmed two of his works, *The Little Minister* and *Quality Street*, during the 1930s. Hepburn's performance in *Sylvia Scarlett* demonstrates that she could have been the greatest Peter Pan of her time.[21] Her Sylvia is an incredibly lovely creature—touched by fantasy, all tomboy grace, mercurial, swift-witted, -tongued, and -tempered. But this Peter Pan is forced to dwell in the real world, and consequently she is touched by melancholy.

Like Sylvia herself, the film becomes caught in the real world. The plot concerns an embezzler who flees from France with his daughter, who wears men's clothing to escape detection. In England they team up with a con man and form a gang of petty thieves and swindlers. For an unexplained reason, Sylvia continues to dress as a boy. Eventually they become tired of the life of crime and all three become strolling players, producing little mimes in the Cornish countryside. The masquerade must end when Sylvia falls in love and must acknowledge herself to be a girl. At this point the film, like Sylvia, has trouble reverting to reality, for it exposes an age-old theatrical conceit, trans-sexual impersonation, with results that it had not sufficiently calculated.

Trans-sexual impersonation is a theatrical convention to which modern thinking has added unfortunate connotations. We can accept it in Shakespeare or in opera because it is a cultural tradition. In modern works it is almost always embarrassing and alienating. Too often it cuts close to our own suspicions about the actor involved or to our fears about ourselves. And frequently the actor shares these same fears with us. *Sylvia Scarlett* runs headlong into this problem. As long as the characters in the play accept the sexual metamorphosis that occurs as part of the magic of a midsummer night, we in the audience can, too. Later in her stage career Hepburn played other *Hosenrollen*, or trouser parts, in *As You Like It* (1950) and *Twelfth Night* (1960), and one is not disturbed as Rosalind becomes Ganymede, or Viola Cesario, and then, as the revels end, resume skirts. The problem in *Sylvia Scarlett* arises when Sylvia becomes caught between two worlds. She can't make it back to being a girl when she falls in love with an artist (played with unbelievable narcissism by Brian Aherne). When the artist no longer wants to paint the boy upon learning that she is a girl, when Sylvia is more mannish in a dress than she was in a suit, when the artist educating the girl to be feminine opens the scene with "Boy! You're a girl!"—the audience is caught on the horns of a dilemma. I doubt if anyone could pull it off, but Hepburn can't manage this part of the role. She gives herself to the part exactly as it is written, but the asexuality that she had achieved in the earlier parts of the role here become distressingly fey.

Sylvia Scarlett is a divided film. The first half, as the preface to the film suggests, is about love and luck, adventure and laughter. The second half brutally states that leading life according to these values is folly. Sylvia has been playing a masquerade, and she can't ring down the curtain when she wants to. Her father goes mad playing a middle-aged juvenile to a fickle soubrette. The artist almost loses Sylvia because he is so immersed in the role of Oberon he is playing to a Russian lady's Titania. The con man suddenly becomes unsavory simply because he continues to treat life as the merry adventure which the film formerly suggested it to be. The effect on the audience is as if it had been invited to a party and then told to go home because it was having too good a time.

Yet *Sylvia Scarlett* is still a film which is endearing for its early charms. Just before the revels end and Sylvia resumes the clothing of a girl, there is a delightful mid-summer idyll complete with Pierrot costumes and evocative, studio-created moonlight. Throughout, the lighting is superb, contributing as here a sense of magic, and, as in the scene showing a crossing of the English Channel, creating a sense of the melodrama and terror that lurk in every young boy's heart as he reads an adventure tale. Van Nest Polglase's settings are equally magical. They appear to be cardboard and canvas—like stage décor—which is very appropriate. A problem arises, as it does in Cukor's later films, when the studio reality of the earlier sets is juxtaposed with the actual outdoor settings (actual but not authentic, since the California coastline is used for Cornwall). There is an attempt to blend sets and locations into a unified whole, but, perhaps because of the schism in the script, one is slightly jarred.

The innocence and magic of *Sylvia Scarlett* is nowhere better exemplified than in a brief musical interlude when Hepburn, Grant, Gwenn, and Dennie Moore, on a wave of euphoria, break into a music-hall rendition of "By the Beautiful Sea." All Cukor's best musical numbers appear in his non-musical films, but none is better than this. This is extravagance, laughter, and adventure. This is what the theater is all about.

Sylvia Scarlett: Dennie Moore, Cary Grant, Katharine Hepburn

Romeo and Juliet: Leslie Howard

Star-Crossed

After *Sylvia Scarlett*, Cukor returned to MGM, this time to work with producer Irving Thalberg. Cukor has said of his relationship with Thalberg:

He was very odd; he was the most charming man and he died at 37—a most gifted man, a real showman. He was very knowledgeable and stimulating for a director. Very often, you work with so-called producers who are just damned nuisances. But Irving would make the most unconventional and interesting suggestions of all kinds. For instance, when we did the parting scene from Romeo and Juliet, *I thought it was very movingly done; and he said, "No . . . no . . . no . . . they're too glum." "But," I said, "Irving, they're parting in the morning." And he said, "No, it could be done, in a sense, with a smile." He didn't mean a mechanical smile; he meant a tenderness, a* chagrin d'amour . . . *a noble and romantic way to say goodbye.*[22]

Romeo and Juliet (1936). Produced by Irving Thalberg for Metro-Goldwyn-Mayer. Based on the play by William Shakespeare, as arranged for the screen by Talbot Jennings. Photographed by William Daniels. Edited by Margaret Booth. With Norma Shearer (Juliet), Leslie Howard (Romeo), John Barrymore (Mercutio), Edna May Oliver (nurse to Juliet), C. Aubrey Smith (Capulet), Basil Rathbone (Tybalt), Andy Devine (Peter), Henry Kolker (Friar Laurence), Violet Kemble-Cooper (Lady Capulet), Ralph Forbes (Paris), Reginald Denny (Benvolio), Maurice Murphy (Balthasar), Conway Tearle (Prince of Verona), Virginia Hammond (Lady Montague), Robert Warwick (Lord Montague), Katherine de Mille (Rosaline).

This film has become such a joke in recent years that it seems hard to believe that at its release it was extremely well received by the critics. Certainly the praise was, in part, offered to the intention rather than to the execution.

Hollywood has rarely seen such an elaborate production—done without any imagination or taste. (Another example that comes to mind is the Dieterle-Reinhardt production of *A Midsummer Night's Dream* in the same year.) This is Hollywood art direction at its worst, and Oliver Messel, a stage director who collaborated with Cedric Gibbons on the sets, exhibited much the same busy-ness in his stage work as he does here, though usually it was checked somewhat by his innate tastefulness. The sets are so fussy, so overly detailed, such a literal-minded creation of fantasy that they imprison the imagination.

Leslie Howard reportedly didn't want to play Romeo because he was too old for the role. This is a problem with filming Shakespeare, because an actor only gains the experience and insight to tackle the playwright's roles at an age when the camera's lens exposes a maturity ill fitted to the part. Still, if Howard were good, I doubt if one would object to his maturity. Howard was never successful playing Shakespeare on the stage; he had diction, but he lacked passion and poetry. Romeo is difficult to play because the character is callow. The quintessence of Howard's personality, his English sensitivity, renders the immaturity of Romeo in an unfortunate way—it brings out the effeminateness latent in the character.

Although Irving Thalberg designed the film as a vehicle for his wife, Norma Shearer, she is patently unequipped to play Juliet. She lacks the diction,[23] the technique, and the passion that the role requires, and the part is hopeless without them; nevertheless she gives herself to the part bravely.

The one member of the cast who was a truly distinguished Shakespearian actor was John Barrymore, playing Mercutio. There is magnetism, presence, and a vocal instrument capable of meeting the demands of Shakespeare's lines. Cukor has recalled that Barrymore conceived Mercutio as a kind of Irish bard, and he rehearsed with his vocal coach by using an Irish brogue. When production began, he stripped the lines of the brogue, so that only the lilt would remain as an underlying rhythm. Unhappily, Barrymore's characterization has a floridness that borders on the faggotty. But if the actor's concept is unsuccessful, his performance still makes one sit up and take notice.

Talbot Jennings' rearrangement of the script for the screen is successful in its attempt for clarity. Owing to the censorship of the times the Rabelaisian quality of the comic interludes has been carefully excised, though one cannot regret the decision considering that these scenes were left in the hands of such actors as Andy Devine and Maurice Murphy. Edna May Oliver seems a clever idea for the nurse, but, in fact, she lacks the note of vicarious lasciviousness that the part must have.

Romeo and Juliet: John Barrymore, Edna May Oliver

Camille: Greta Garbo

Garbo

About his choice of material Cukor has said:
In the old days, the studios were so wonderfully organized;
they had seventy-five writers, and they had great talent
. . . they bought everything. It was all done for you, and
I never appreciated all the things they did for one. As I
remember, one was given a choice. For example, when
they said—after it had been determined that I was to do
a picture with Garbo—would I like to do Manon Lescaut
or The Lady of the Camellias? *And I said, "Oh, I'd love*
to do The Lady of the Camellias" *because I'd always had*
a hunch about that. You were given certain choices, but
the things were originated by the studio. You could bring
some material to them if it interested you very much. '. . .
I don't know who suggested Little Women, *but the point is*
that when they did, I took fire. The same happened with
David Copperfield. *But if I'd been lackadaisical, it would*
not have gone forward.[24]

Cukor's hunch about Garbo and *Camille* proved to be
right on target. *Manon* is a finer work of literature, and
it had the advantage of less exposure, but Manon is not
a role that is well suited to Garbo. Manon has to be about
sixteen years old at the beginning of the story, and she
is in her early twenties at the end. Marguerite Gautier,
the heroine of *Camille*, is supposed to be in her early
twenties also, but it is a role whose credibility is not
weakened when played by a more mature actress (Garbo
was thirty-one when the film was made). Also Manon
is really a tramp, destroying most of the men who love
her, and her ending is sordid. The role offers none of the
dignity or self-sacrifice that are such essential parts of
Garbo's on-screen personality. Clearly, of the two roles,
Marguerite is better suited to Garbo.

Camille (1937). Produced by David Lewis for Metro-
Goldwyn-Mayer. Script by Zoë Akins, Frances Marion,

and James Hilton, from the play and the novel, *La Dame aux camélias* by Alexandre Dumas fils. Photographed by William Daniels and Karl Freund. Edited by Margaret Booth. With Greta Garbo (Marguerite Gautier), Robert Taylor (Armand Duval), Lionel Barrymore (M. Duval), Jessie Ralph (Nanine), Henry Daniell (Baron de Varville), Laura Hope Crews (Prudence), Rex O'Malley (Gaston), Lenore Ulric (Olympe), Elizabeth Allan (Nichette).

Garbo's Marguerite Gautier is the single most beautiful performance in the American sound film. The force of its intelligence and delicacy fills us with the awe and admiration awarded the great legendary actresses of the past. We respond not merely to great acting, though assuredly this *is* great acting, but rather to some supreme intensity of personality, so pure that we are mystified and exalted. In other times, and possibly for less, actresses were called "divine." With the force of recognition, we *feel* the meaning of the epithet.

The physical attractions of actors seem to embarrass critics so that they rarely speak of them, although if they were candid, they would admit that often their judgments are based on this factor. One can't discuss Garbo without touching on her beauty because it is the cornerstone of many of her performances. This is particularly true in *Camille*, for the suffering inherent in the role seems to complete her beauty. She is herself a work of art.

In no other film does Garbo act so effectively with her body. In the scene with Armand's father, when Marguerite knows she is defeated, she sinks to the floor, one hand holding the table. It is admirable; it has something of the quality of Pavlova's dying swan about it. But it is not really balletic, for it is an actress's movement, predicated upon an instinctive awareness of what the character would do. Equally remarkable is the movement she makes to pick

Camille: Lenore Ulric, Laura Hope Crews, Greta Garbo
Camille: Greta Garbo, Henry Daniell, Lenore Ulric, Robert Taylor

up her fan when the Baron de Varville refuses to retrieve it for her. It is done in one complete movement, seemingly without bending her knees. It should be awkward, but somehow Garbo achieves an effect of the purest dignity.

Nowhere, however, is this physical control so breathtaking as in the final scene. As she lies on her bed, clothed in a robe that suggests a shroud, her body, barely able to support the smile she wears when she sees Armand, has an ethereal weightlessness. There seems to be not an ounce of strength in her body; to touch the camellias Gaston has brought her seems a herculean task. At the very end, as Armand holds her, her face, stripped of make-up, the skin translucent, becomes ecstatic. Her death scene succeeds in conveying what no other actor I have seen has been able to attain: a sense of the life slipping away and the weight of the body being shed.

Garbo imbues every moment, even the light and flirting ones, with an inner sadness, with an awareness of mortality, and with the understanding such an awareness has given her; there is a touch of the mystic about her performance. In a curious way she seems to fulfill the portrait that Alexandre Dumas tried to capture of the true Marguerite Gautier, his mistress, Marie Duplessis.

Garbo's performance has been criticized for being too sublime. This is because there is a misconception of the courtesans of the nineteenth century. They were not streetwalkers; those who rose to the top of their profession had to acquire at least the veneer of refinement. I doubt if any of them, even Marie Duplessis, attained the dignity that Garbo gives Marguerite Gautier, but the interpretation is not so wide of the mark as the modern misconception of the courtesan implies.

Cukor's influence on Garbo's Marguerite cannot be measured. Beyond blocking out the scenes and creating a conducive atmosphere for the actress, Cukor perhaps did very little.[25] There is such deep communication between actress and role that one feels sure the conception is entirely intuitive. With such a performance, the director can act only as an editor, maintaining the proper shadings, deleting a gesture here, suggesting one elsewhere.

Cukor credits much of the power of Garbo's performance to a certain boldness in her thinking which fills the silences and supports the action and dialogue:

I find that people who leave their mark are bold and uncensored in the way they think. . . . Now, for example, in Camille *there was a scene where Armand left a party—the most extraordinarily erotic and titillating scene. Garbo had her hands at her sides, and she kissed Armand on his face, all over; and it generated the most extraordinary eroticism. And that's because she was thinking certain things; and that's what did it—thinking boldly and without fear and without censorship.*[26]

Aside from Garbo's performance, there is little to say about the film. The screenplay, which Cukor credits almost entirely to Zoë Akins, is well constructed and smooth, particularly successful in creating a period dialogue that doesn't jar. Throughout the film there runs a streak of vulgarity, especially in the acting of the supporting cast. Particularly offensive are Laura Hope Crews and Lenore Ulric as Marguerite's courtesan friends, Prudence and Olympe. Though the role of Armand is a thankless one, Robert Taylor brings to it a callowness that makes one wonder what Marguerite saw in him. The answer to that question is Henry Daniell's dour performance as the Baron de Varville, her former lover.

The sets were carefully researched, but the result was such an accumulation of detail that everything seems a bit too tarted-up for Garbo's Marguerite. It's a fussy production that gives us back the play as it is popularly conceived—lush, rich, and vulgar.

Great plays can withstand any interpretation, as most productions of Shakespeare prove. Others gain their vitality only when the absolutely correct interpreter comes along to transcend the material. *Camille* is one of these. Stark Young in reviewing a 1926 production of *La Dame aux camélias* remarked, "All it needs is the soul of a great artist to give it life and significance."[27] Garbo has the soul, and the play lives in her significance.

Cukor's only other experience in directing Garbo was the notorious *Two-Faced Woman,* four years later. This was the film that caused Garbo to choose exile from motion pictures. Garbo's career, more than that of any other actor, was affected strongly by the war in Europe. Her films depended upon the European market to return a profit—few, if any, of her films made money from their domestic exhibition alone. MGM was, for the first time, faced with the challenge of producing a Garbo film that would show a profit from its American distribution alone. They ruled out the lush romantic vehicles in which the actress had specialized and chose for her a frothy comedy. The script was based on a tired Hungarian play which had already seen service as a Constance Talmadge vehicle, *Her Sister from Paris* (1925). *Two-Faced Woman* is little more than a variation of Ferenc Molnár's *The Guardsman* with the sexes reversed: a wife thinks her husband may be unfaithful, so she invents a twin sister to tempt him down the garden path. One sister is sportsy and clean-living; the other is a flirt and a playgirl.

MGM's publicity campaign announced a new Garbo. It was emphasized that she would appear in a bathing suit, dance, swim, and ski, sport a new bobbed hairdo, and in general carry on like the typical all-American girl. Garbo had misgivings; she commented succinctly, "They're trying to kill me."

Camille: Greta Garbo, Robert Taylor
Two-Faced Woman: Greta Garbo, Melvyn Douglas

When the film was released, it ran into serious trouble. Because of its suggestion of adultery, it was condemned by the National Legion of Decency. MGM hastily withdrew the film from distribution, made a few cuts, and added a scene in which it becomes clear that the husband is on to his wife's plot from the start, thus erasing even the suspicion of adultery. The moralists were assuaged but the critics were not. The film received poor reviews, and Garbo decided to retire from films until the end of the war, when her European market could again be tapped.

Two-Faced Woman (1941). Produced by Gottfried Reinhardt for Metro-Goldwyn-Mayer. Script by S. N. Behrman, Salka Viertel, and George Oppenheimer, from a play by Ludwig Fulda. Photographed by Joseph Ruttenberg. Edited by George Boemler. With Greta Garbo (Karin Borg, Katherin Borg), Melvyn Douglas (Larry Blake), Constance Bennett (Griselda Vaughan), Robert Sterling (Dick Williams), Roland Young (Oscar Miller), Ruth Gordon (Ruth Ellis).

Considering all the contumely heaped on *Two-Faced Woman,* it is a surprise to find that it is a rather pleasant, if forgettable, comedy. Reportedly there was never a finished script for this film, and it does have the feeling of the slapdash and the jerry-built. Nonetheless there are a number of amusing scenes.

A skillful supporting cast helps camouflage the fact that the film can't quite maintain the high spirits for which it tries: Melvyn Douglas' blandness has a suavity that makes him easy to take; Ruth Gordon gives one of her rare, controlled, *sensible* performances in film; best of all is Constance Bennett, who plays Garbo's rival with living bitchiness and a drooling venom that makes her lines seem almost high comedy. A frivolous, light comedienne— such as Claudette Colbert or Carole Lombard—might have made the film really enjoyable. There is a heaviness about Garbo's voice that makes it wrong for comedy playing; her timing is off a beat; the light touch seems alien to her Nordic temperament. The attempt to Americanize her appearance also fails. It emphasizes the harsh, rawboned quality that she sometimes exhibited. Over all there is a sense of strain in the performance, and we become aware that the actress is ill-at-ease within the role.

Though *Ninotchka* has been used to prove the opposite, I doubt if Garbo possessed comic skills. *Ninotchka* is an extremely cleverly written script which develops comedy partly from the fact that its leading actress has little sense of humor. When she is awakened by love, she is infused with romantic intensity rather than comic warmth. Garbo's playing in the later scenes demands only a slightly lighter emphasis than her usual romantic portrayal. In *Two-Faced Woman* the script is not so skillful, for it asks Garbo to play with a lightness of touch that is not hers. Nor does the character allow her to show the disillusioned but still impassioned acceptance of life which dignified previous roles of equal inconsequence.

Holiday: Lew Ayres, Katharine Hepburn

Miss Hepburn and Mr. Barry

Playwright Philip Barry and actress Katharine Hepburn have a long and checkered career of involvement. One of Hepburn's first jobs in the theater was as the understudy for the lead in Barry's play, *Holiday*, in 1928. She was also cast as one of the two female leads in Barry's 1932 play *The Animal Kingdom*, but there were disagreements during the play's rehearsals, and she was fired.

For her screen test for the role in *A Bill of Divorcement*, Hepburn chose a scene from *Holiday*. In 1938, when her career had begun to wane, she bought her release from RKO studios in order to have autonomy in choosing her film roles. According to Cukor, it was her idea to remake *Holiday* (it had already been filmed once in 1931), and it was she who convinced Columbia to produce it. Obviously, she felt an affinity for the role of Linda Seton and hoped the film would turn the tide for her career.

It didn't, for in the same year she was labeled "box-office poison." (This makes no sense, since *Holiday* was one of the top-grossing films for the same year.) When the film was finished, Hepburn left Hollywood with no definite plans. It was to be two years before she returned to the screen, and in the comeback Barry would play a major role.

Holiday (1938). Produced by Everett Riskin for Columbia Pictures. Script by Donald Ogden Stewart and Sidney Buchman, from the play by Philip Barry. Photographed by Franz Planer. Edited by Otto Meyer and Al Clark. With Katharine Hepburn (Linda Seton), Cary Grant (Johnny Case), Doris Nolan (Julia Seton), Lew Ayres (Ned Seton), Edward Everett Horton (Nick Potter), Jean Dixon (Susan Potter), Henry Daniell (Seton Cram), Binnie Barnes (Laura Cram), Henry Kolker (Edward Seton).

Holiday is Philip Barry's finest play and Cukor's loveliest film. It shimmers with grace, intelligence, and humor,
and it is laced with deep feeling. Its story is quintessen-
tially Barry. Johnny Case, a boy from the wrong side
of the tracks, falls in love with the wealthy Julia Seton.
Julia presumes that Johnny will naturally accept a job in
her father's bank, but Johnny has another future in mind,
and, though he's not sure what it will be, it doesn't re-
volve around such a stuffy, money-making job. Julia's
sister, Linda, the black sheep of the family, supports
Johnny in his fight against her family's intolerant style
of life. Linda, of course, ends up with Johnny.

Barry's play is a romantic comedy, but like many of the
better comedies of the twenties and early thirties, it has
a serious undercurrent. Barry is criticizing the materialism
of American life, and the snobbishness and stultification
that can result from a money-oriented society. The play
has an inherent flaw in that one is not too sure about
the sincerity of Johnny Case's revolt. There is the faint
aroma of the bounder about it. There is also a touch of
the 1920s aesthete who had an inverse snobbism toward
the philistine. Johnny's credibility depends upon the actor's ability to charm us into believing the seriousness of
his intentions. Cary Grant succeeds.

Linda Seton, the play's central character, is as critical
of the society in which she lives as is Johnny, but she is
also a product of that society. To it she owes the breeding,
the elegance, and the poise that only the background of
money can supply. Her innate intelligence and sensitivity,
however, are at odds with the shallow and stultified circle
of family and acquaintances who surround her. Without
Johnny, Linda might never have escaped that life of
frustration that has already immobilized her equally fine,
but weaker, brother Ned. With Johnny, she escapes—
although neither is sure exactly what they may find.

Their chance lies in finding the affirmation of that better life they may have only nebulously formulated but nevertheless passionately believe is possible.

The quality of *Holiday* springs from the fervor of its optimism and the vibrancy with which Linda affirms it. From hindsight, we can feel condescending toward its naïveté, and it is true that *Holiday* is very much the product of its time. In 1938 the film was criticized for being out of step with the mood of a nation not yet out of a depression and close to a war. *Holiday,* nonetheless, is an affecting play because of the purity and vigor of the author's belief in what he is saying. Barry's later plays suffer from an attitude of despair. About this time, Barry began to write straight dramatic plays that failed because he became trapped in the labyrinth of his own confusion. He was a comic writer who found that there was no time for comedy, and his later comedies such as *The Philadelphia Story* are synthetic. They try to recapture the spirit of *Holiday,* but the author himself no longer really believes in it.

The dialogue of Barry's early romantic comedies is highly individual. It is a kind of elegant banter, but under it is an abruptness and tension that suggests that the characters are withholding more than they are telling. A sample is this scene (which is incorporated into the movie *in toto*) between Linda and her alcoholic brother:

Linda: *What's it like to get drunk, Ned?*

Ned: *It's. . . . How drunk?*

Linda: *Good and drunk.*

Ned: *Grand.*

Linda: How *is it?*

Ned: *Well, to begin with, it brings you to life.*

Linda: *Does it?*

Ned: *Yes . . . and after a while you begin to know all about it. You feel . . . I don't know . . . important.*

Linda: *That must be good.*

Ned: *It is. Then pretty soon the game starts.*

Linda: *What game?*

Ned: *That game you play with yourself. It's a swell game . . . there's not a sweller game on this earth really.*

Linda: *How does it go?*

Ned: *Well, you think clear as crystal, but every move, every sentence is a problem. That—gets pretty interesting.*

Linda: *I see.*

Ned: *Swell game. Most terribly exciting game.*

Linda: *You . . . get beaten though, don't you.*

Ned: *Sure. But that's alright, too. Then you don't mind anything . . . not anything at all. Then you sleep.*

Linda: *How long can you keep it up?*

Ned: *A long while. As long as you last.*

Linda: *Oh, Ned! That's awful!*

Ned: *Think so? Other things are worse.*

Linda: *But . . . but where do you end up?*

Ned: *Where everyone ends up. You die . . . and that's alright, too.*

Linda: *Ned, can you do it on champagne?*

Ned: *Why . . . what's the matter, Linda?*

Linda: *Nothing.*

Ned: *I know.*

Linda: *Yes?*

Ned: *Johnny?*

Linda: *Give me some more wine, Ned.*

Ned: *He's a funny guy, isn't he.*

Linda: *Give me some more, Ned . . .*

Ned: *You can tell me about it, dear . . .*

Linda: *I love the boy, Neddy . . .*

Ned: *I thought so . . . Hell, isn't it?*

Linda: *I guess it will be.*

Holiday: Doris Nolan, Cary Grant, Katharine Hepburn
Holiday:
Jean Dixon, Katharine Hepburn, Lew Ayres, Edward Everett Horton

The scene is meant to be played lightly. The relatively short lines which dovetail so beautifully have a swift rhythm which does not allow the underlying emotion to surface. When it does, as Linda says, "I love the boy, Neddy," the impact is overwhelming. Then as soon as the emotion is out, the bantering tone is swiftly resumed. Barry's gift for dialogue was just this: writing light, airy lines that were nonetheless supercharged with emotion.

The scene quoted above (which is the one Hepburn used for her screen test for *A Bill of Divorcement*) is quite the loveliest in all American film comedies of the thirties. Hepburn and Lew Ayres (who plays Ned) are extremely sensitive to the demands of the text, and they play with elegant fluidity, tenderness, and great sensibility.

Holiday exemplifies the type of comedy at which Cukor is best. There is a strong human situation at its center and strong characters that can be developed and are worth his camera's time spent lingering over them. There is not a single misplaced camera set-up or ill-judged cut in the film. The film can be faulted only on two points. First, there is the art direction. A character in the film describes the Seton home as Grand Central Station; one imagines thas was meant to be an exaggeration, but the finished film makes it literally true. Also some of the minor characters are badly cast. It is loading one's guns a little too much to cast such sour, disagreeable actors as Henry Daniell and Henry Kolker as the unlikeable Setons. Doris Nolan's uninteresting beauty is no foil for the distictiveness of Hepburn's personality. No Johnny Case worth his salt would look twice at this Julia after he had met Hepburn's Linda.

In all other areas, Cukor is extremely fortunate in his collaborators. The titles give credit for the screenplay to both Donald Ogden Stewart and Sidney Buchman, but Cukor says that it was Stewart's work completely. Stewart played in the original Broadway company of *Holiday,* and he is extremely sympathetic to Barry. Though the play has been opened up for the screen, Stewart retained the best of Barry's dialogue almost without change. The alterations he made strengthen the script. He virtually rewrote the parts of Susan and Nick Potter, making them warmer and more sympathetic characters (beautifully played by Edward Everett Horton and, particularly, Jean Dixon who retired from the screen after this performance). These characters are so in tune with the original script that it is a surprise to learn that they are more Stewart's creation than Barry's.

The film's strongest point is Hepburn's performance. The part was written for Hope Williams, a theater star of the time, to whom Hepburn was often compared in her early career because of a similarity in their abrupt and boyish manner of playing. The character of Linda Seton coincides precisely with Hepburn's abilities as an actress. Both character and actress are by nature patrician; both are gifted with a shining intelligence—indeed, intelligence is the primary component of Hepburn's image; both are forceful. There is an edge of hypertension in Hepburn's acting that makes her ideal for playing women whose finest characteristics or ideals have been, for whatever reason, inhibited or frustrated.

In the long run, for all the analysis in the world, the precise element that makes Hepburn's performance the lovely thing that it is remains elusive. Just as Barry's belief in Linda Seton colors the writing of the role, so in some intangible way does Hepburn's admiration for the character and the play shine through her performance.

Soon after the completion of *Holiday,* Hepburn left Hollywood and went to her family's home in Connecticut, with no definite plans about her career. While she was there, Philip Barry got in touch with her and outlined a new play, *The Philadelphia Story,* he was writing, in which he hoped she might be interested in playing. Further conversations ensued at Barry's summer home in Maine, and the character of Tracy was molded to fit Hepburn's personality. The play opened in New York on March 26, 1939, with a supporting company that included Van Heflin, Joseph Cotten, and Shirley Booth. It was such a huge success that it guaranteed the continued existence of its producer, the Theatre Guild, which up to this time had been seriously in the red.

Prior to the New York opening, Hepburn had bought the film rights to the play. Later she sold these to Metro-Goldwyn-Mayer with certain stipulations: she was to play the part of Tracy on the screen; she was to have Cukor as her director; and she was to have approval of her leading men and of the scriptwriter. Cukor saw the stage production many times and took copious notes, with particular attention to those moments which showed Hepburn to advantage. For leading men, Hepburn chose James Stewart and Cary Grant to bolster her pull at the box-office. As scriptwriter she chose Donald Ogden Stewart. The film was possibly an even greater success than the play, and Hepburn had so masterfully planned her own comeback that she was admired as much for her business acumen as for her performance.

The Philadelphia Story (1940). Produced by Joseph L. Mankiewicz for Metro-Goldwyn-Mayer. Script by Donald Ogden Stewart from the play by Philip Barry. Photographed by Joseph Ruttenberg. Edited by Frank Sullivan. With Katharine Hepburn (Tracy Lord), Cary Grant (C. K. Dexter Haven), James Stewart (Mike Connor), Ruth Hussey (Liz Imbrie), John Howard (George Kittredge), Roland Young (Uncle Willie), John Halliday (Seth Lord),

The Philadelphia Story:
Cary Grant, Katharine Hepburn, James Stewart
The Philadelphia Story: John Howard, Katharine Hepburn

Virginia Weidler (Dinah Lord), Mary Nash (Margaret Lord), Henry Daniell (Sidney Kidd).

"Shaw exposes the condition of women, Barrie exalts the virtue of ladies, Maugham exhibits the vices of females, Barry exploits the talents of actresses." So says a pedantic theater buff in James Thurber's story, "Get Thee to a Monastery," published 1954. Thurber's character presumably refers to the playwright's career from the time of *The Philadelphia Story*. With this play and those that follow, there is a definite decline in Barry's work. His only important plays were another and distinctly mediocre vehicle for Hepburn, *Without Love* (1942) and a vehicle for Tallulah Bankhead, *Foolish Notion* (1945). These plays, and I include *The Philadelphia Story,* are distinctly disappointing, however enjoyable sitting through them may at the time seem, because they are synthetic. Though skillfully constructed, with cleverly written dialogue, the playwright seems concerned only with practicing his craft. These are the plays of a man with a talent to amuse but without the ability to make his audiences care beyond the play's duration.

What is really displeasing about *The Philadelphia Story* is the cleverness with which it popularizes Hepburn's image. This image was always perhaps a little too rarefied for most taste, and *The Philadelphia Story* discovers a way to bring her down to earth. Her character, Tracy Lord, is told off in no uncertain terms by practically everyone in the play, and in the end she is brought down to the level of those around her. If one looks carefully at the script, one finds that the things Tracy won't tolerate are invasion of privacy, her ex-husband's alcoholism, and her father's infidelity with a chorus cutie. The three great women stars of 1930s films all had their comeuppance when the taste in heroines turned to clean-cut girls next door: Marlene Dietrich had to wrestle and be roughed up in *Destry Rides Again*; Garbo became sportsy in *Two-Faced Woman*; and Hepburn learned how to be a "first class human being" in *The Philadelphia Story*. Of these transformations, Hepburn's was the most successful, and she was to repeat it many times: the ice princess who turns to flesh under the right touch. Hepburn plays Tracy Lord as she was to play the subsequent carbon copies, with great comic flair. But it is not really attractive to see many of her most distinctive qualities—her aristocratic demeanor, her intelligence, her inner-directedness—played against her equally natural warmth and charm. It is the combination of these two sides of her personality that make her one of the most distinctive personalities in film, and she is at her best, as in *Holiday*, when they can exist harmoniously within the character.

The screen adaptation of *The Philadelphia Story* was done with extreme skill by Donald Ogden Stewart. Though a few minor scenes are entirely the work of Stewart (and again there is a perfect unity of writing style), he has mainly rearranged certain scenes to open up the play to include more settings. Cukor's direction is highly polished, and, as usual when he is at his best, one is absolutely unaware of technique. Toward the end there is a take lasting almost three minutes between Katharine Hepburn and Cary Grant, but the actors are good enough and the scene strong enough to hold our attention.

Cukor has also achieved a real sense of concord, almost of ensemble playing, among the actors. They are uniformly excellent, though James Stewart's performance might be better with less charm and more abrasiveness, particularly in the early part of the film. Cary Grant is ideal as C. K. Dexter Haven—his personality has just the right combination of the flippant and the sincere for the role. In fact, this is not a film that one can fault strongly in any department. The fault lies in the original material.

The Women: Joan Crawford

The Crawford Years

After he had been removed from *Gone with the Wind,*
Cukor was assigned to bring Clare Boothe's highly successful comedy, *The Women,* to the screen. This was another of those stage vehicles which, like *Dinner at Eight,*
was made for the Hollywood all-star treatment. *The
Women* presented certain problems, since its dialogue
contained a number of lines that were, for the screen,
too risqué. Anita Loos, who was one of the adaptors
of the play for the screen, told me that her main chore was
to paraphrase Miss Boothe's witticisms into cleaner *bons
mots.* For Cukor, the film presented the problem of being
ringmaster for a great number of Hollywood's leading
ladies. Joan Crawford, who had been the reigning glamour queen at MGM, was facing a crisis in her career—
encroaching middle-age—and she realized that she must
branch out if her career was to continue to blossom. She
wanted the role of Crystal, the tartish perfume saleswoman, who steals the heroine's husband. Crawford had
worked once before with Cukor when he replaced the
sick Edward Griffith on *No More Ladies,* though he received no credit. She found him a hard taskmaster. She
respected Cukor, and when neither Louis B. Mayer nor
producer Hunt Stromberg wanted her for the part, she
approached the director who convinced everyone that she
should play Crystal.

The Women (1939). Produced by Hunt Stromberg for
Metro-Goldwyn-Mayer. Script by Anita Loos and Jane
Murfin, from the play by Clare Boothe. Photographed by
Oliver T. Marsh and Joseph Ruttenberg. Edited by Robert
J. Kern. With Norma Shearer (Mary Haines), Joan Craw-
ford (Crystal Allen), Rosalind Russell (Sylvia Fowler),
Mary Boland (Flora de Lave), Paulette Goddard (Miriam
Aarons), Joan Fontaine (Peggy Day), Virginia Weidler
(Mary), Marjorie Main (Lucy), Lucile Watson (Mrs.

Morehead), Phyllis Povah (Edith Potter), Ruth Hussey (Miss Watts), Margaret Dumont (Miss Wagstaff), Dennie Moore (Olga), Esther Dale (Ingrid), Hedda Hopper (Dolly Dupuyster), Florence Nash (Nancy Blake), Ann Morriss (Exercise Instructress), Mary Beth Hughes (Miss Trimmerback), Virginia Grey (Pat), Cora Witherspoon (Mrs. Van Adams), Aileen Pringle (Dress Saleswoman), Judith Allen (Model).

Cukor might have been answering those critics who complained of his slow pacing when he staged the opening sequence of *The Women,* for it is all swift-moving camera, fast cuts, and half-caught dialogue until it stops as Sylvia Fowler (Rosalind Russell) hears the piece of gossip that sets the whole episodic plot in motion. We never hear the story because it is drowned out by a hair dryer. It is a long film (132 minutes), but Cukor keeps it moving smartly. In a very short time we are introduced to a wealth of characters, whom we are expected to catch on the run. The characters have no substance, so if we miss what they say or do at first, we can catch it the next time around. Each of the characters is introduced by a title that depicts her as an animal—Mary is a doe; Sylvia a cat; Miriam a fox; etc.—and indeed the film goes no further in deepening these cartoon characterizations.

In her introduction to the published play, Miss Boothe had written, "*The Women* is a satirical play about a numerically small group of ladies native to the Park Avenues of America." I think Miss Boothe overrates the quality of her writing if she truly considers it satire, for *The Women* is written with the mind, heart, and style of a female gossip columnist. Bitchy humor, if it is top drawer, can be quite amusing, but some of Miss Boothe's lines are rather thin. For example:

Come on, Countess, chin up! Both of them!

He says, "I gotta go home tomorrow, baby!" And I

The Women: Joan Fontaine, Rosalind Russell,
Florence Nash, Phyllis Povah
Susan and God: Rita Hayworth, Joan Crawford, John Carroll

says, "Why?" And he says, "My family always expects me home on Easter." So I says, "What do they expect you to do? Lay an egg?"

I'd love to do Mrs. Fowler's nails, right down to the wrist, with a nice big buzz saw.

Somehow this dialogue seems more suitable to a wise-cracking gold-diggers movie of the early thirties than to a smash Broadway comedy.

Most of the ladies of the cast undertake Miss Boothe's venom with relish. Probably the most famous performance in the film is that of Rosalind Russell as Sylvia Fowler, the arch-bitch of all time. Never for one moment does Sylvia Fowler resemble any living woman (for in real life no one would put up with her); still Miss Russell swoops down on the role with such predatoriness that she turns a monstrous caricature into a flesh-and-blood freak. Norma Shearer gives her all to the insipid gentility of the one nice character, but she gets rather carried away at the end when she rushes into her husband's arms with that same ecstasy she supplied for Juliet's death scene.

As Crystal, Joan Crawford is quite good. She plays the role exactly as it is written—cheap, hard as nails, and with no sense of humor, but Miss Boothe has not written a credible character. No man, no matter how badly he was suffering from the seven-year itch, would fall for this tramp.

As a novelty, *The Women* included one color sequence of a fashion show. It is more of a mini-revue than a fashion show, but the fantasy of Adrian's clothes (here and throughout the film) are burlesqued with good humor and affection. One wishes that Miss Boothe's original script had a little more of both qualities.

MGM bought Rachel Crothers' hit play, *Susan and God,* for Norma Shearer. Miss Shearer, however, didn't want to play the part of the mother of a teen-aged daughter and turned down the film. Cukor suggested Joan Crawford for the role, and she jumped at the chance to play a part created on the stage by Gertrude Lawrence.

Susan and God (1939). Produced by Hunt Stromberg for Metro-Goldwyn-Mayer. Script by Anita Loos, from the play by Rachel Crothers. Photographed by Robert Planck. Edited by William H. Terhune. With Joan Crawford (Susan Trexel), Fredric March (Barrie Trexel), Ruth Hussey (Charlotte Marley), Nigel Bruce (Hutchins Stubbs), Ruth Quigley (Blossom Trexel), Rose Hobart (Irene Burroughs), Bruce Cabot (Michael O'Hara), Rita Hayworth (Leonora Stubbs), John Carroll (Clyde Rochester), Constance Collier (Lady Wigstaff), Marjorie Main (Mary), Gloria De Haven (Enid).

In the early 1920s Rachel Crothers played an important role in shaping the American comedy of manners. Many of her plays dealt with the problems the modern woman faced in emancipating herself from the shackles of "nice" society; some of these plays—*Nice People* (1921), *Mary the Third* (1923), and *Let Us Be Gay* (1929)—are still very readable today. By the late 1930s, much of this battle had been won and Miss Crothers' plays begin to dwindle in force. *Susan and God* is almost an about face from the earlier plays: its heroine is criticized for putting her ideals before her family. Susan's ideals however, are those of a religious quack, and she herself is a silly, vain, frivolous woman, and the issue of the play is no issue at all. Miss Crothers was, nonetheless, an able craftsman, and undoubtedly the comedy played well on stage.

In adapting the play for the screen, Anita Loos cut away a lot of the dead wood of the tiresome subplots, strengthened the roles of the father and the daughter to equal the importance of Susan's role, and added a number of funny scenes entirely of her own devising (including a role not in the play for Cukor's friend Constance Collier). By concentrating on the family relationships, Miss Loos gave a more human quality to the story than it had in the play, which must have had Cukor's approval, whether or not it was he who suggested it.

According to the contemporary reviews, the play had been staged by Miss Crothers with lightning speed. Once again Cukor was criticized for slackening the pace and the film does dawdle a bit over the domesticity of mother, father, and daughter. Nonetheless, one of the early scenes, when Susan begins to force her new-found religion on a group of friends, is a model of staging a play before the camera. It is a long sequence incorporating practically all of the second half of the play's first act, and it uses many cuts and angles, as well as camera movements, with unerring judgments as to where the spectator's eye would rest within the stage picture, whether on the complete ensemble, on groups of two or three, or on a single person. So precise is Cukor's instinct, and so discreet are the movements and editing, that one is aware only of a complete unit of action.

Joan Crawford gives a skillful carbon copy of the performance Gertrude Lawrence must have given on stage. All that is missing from Crawford's performance is charm and the vitality of the original creation. Without charm Susan becomes a tiresome, vain, selfish woman, and the play falls apart.

The rest of the cast is more than competent except for Rita Hayworth, John Carroll, and Bruce Cabot who seem to be bit players hired for the occasion because they own the right clothes. The real joy of the film is Marjorie Main in the role of the caretaker, another part that is entirely Miss Loos's creation. It is worth watching the movie merely to see what Miss Main can do with a simple line like, "The room was painted last spring, Susan."

It was Joan Crawford's idea to make the film *A Woman's Face*, which was based on a French play and had been made in Sweden as *En kvinnas ansikte* starring Ingrid Bergman. Crawford saw in the property a chance for the dramatic triumph that she felt her career at this point needed. Though MGM did not feel it was wise for their glamour girl to play a badly scarred woman, Crawford gained Cukor's support, and they eventually sold the idea to Louis Mayer.

Joan Crawford has recalled some of Cukor's direction during the shooting of *A Woman's Face*:

What worried George Cukor was my emotionalism. He anticipated that wearing a scar could affect me as wearing a cape has been known to affect some actors. To offset the possibility, he rehearsed the very life out of me. Hours of drilling, with camera and lights lined up for the opening sequence in the courtroom, then *Mr. Cukor had me recite the multiplication table by twos until all emotion was drained and I was totally exhausted, my voice dwindled to a tired monotone.* "Now," *Mr. Cukor said.* "Now, Anna . . . tell us the story of your life."[28]

A Woman's Face (1941). Produced by Victor Saville for Metro-Goldwyn-Mayer. Script by Donald Ogden Stewart and Elliott Paul, based on the play *Il était une fois* by Francis de Croisset. Photographed by Robert Planck. Edited by Frank Sullivan. With Joan Crawford (Anna Holm), Melvyn Douglas (Dr. Gustave Segert), Conrad Veidt (Torsten Barring), Osa Massen (Vera Magnus Barring), Marjorie Main (Emma Kristiansdotter), Connie Gilchrist (Christina Dalvik), Donald Meek (Herman Rundvik), Richard Nichols (Lars-Eric).

Anna Holm's story is not a pretty one. Scarred hideously on one side of her face, she has withdrawn to the shadowy Swedish underworld where she heads a gang of black-mailers. The role of Anna Holm forecasts the parts Craw-ford would specialize in during the late forties and fifties following her "triumph" in *Mildred Pierce*—those hard-as-nails dames who fight to get where they're going against tremendous melodramatic odds. *A Woman's Face* is no less absurd then many of the later vehicles—there is something of the cosmetician's viewpoint about this story of a wicked girl who reforms after her scar is removed—but it has a little more bite and dramatic weight to it. It's certainly the most effective film of that curious subdivision of the Hollywood melodrama, plastic surgery.

The film is flawed by retaining the Swedish setting. There really is no reason why the story could not have been Americanized and had it been, certain absurdities could have been avoided. Though a few members of the cast are Europeans, the majority are not, nor do they make any attempt to appear so. There is an uproarious Swedish folk dance that, for all I know, may be authentic, but to see Joan Crawford hoofing it in a cone-shaped hat, vest, flowered apron, and woolen skirt does not carry conviction.

Joan Crawford is effective, fully using her imposing presence, and under Cukor's tutelage she exhibits a degree of warmth that is rare in her performances. Cukor also succeeds in giving the film a European look—the lighting is particularly helpful in this regard. Cukor gives much of the credit for the production to the producer Victor Saville:

There was a funicular railroad or something that was done in cuts and process; and things that are absolutely brilliant that I shot, but it was all planned and laid out by Victor Saville. There were chases in the snow; and then,

*there was a scene in a waterfall and that was absolutely
dazzling and quite wonderful. They were done by A.
Arnold Gillespie at Special Effects.*[29]

Cukor's direction is sound, but he lacks that note of
perversity and cruelty that a director such as Fritz Lang
or Joseph Losey might have supplied. He doesn't emphasize the seediness of the blackmailer's lair or properly
relish the constant taunting that the scarred woman must
endure. He accepts the script at face value rather than
attempting to transform it into a stylistic exercise in the
perverse.

A Woman's Face: Melvyn Douglas, Joan Crawford

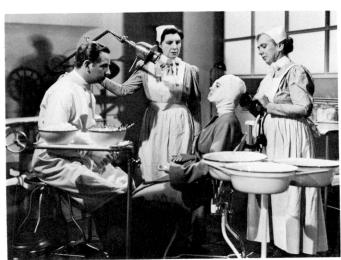

Gaslight: Charles Boyer, Ingrid Bergman

Vamping Till Ready

The forties were not a good period for Cukor. For whatever reason, he did not get the scripts nor the actors that
encouraged his best work. It was not until Cukor worked
with the scripts written by Ruth Gordon and Garson
Kanin in the early fifties and with Judy Holliday and
Hepburn and Tracy that he again found congenial actors
and material.

The forties and fifties were a period of tough broads
and girls next door, ordinary Joes, private eyes, and
criminals. It was a noticeably bad period for comedy.
There was a definite trend toward realism—mistakenly
identified with the ordinary, the small emotions, the
photographic reality. The small TV drama and European
neo-realism contributed to the new outlook. At the same
time came appropriate acting, the Method, a reinterpreta-
tion by the Actors Studio in New York of the system of
Stanislavski. The Method produced a number of admirable actors, but it failed to give them the technique, the
vocal equipment, the tradition, or the understanding to
cope with anything but contemporary realistic drama.

Cukor was understandably not at home.

Her Cardboard Lover (1942). Produced by J. Walter
Rubin for Metro-Goldwyn-Mayer. Script by John Collier,
Anthony Veiller, William H. Wright, and Jacques Deval,
from the play by Deval. Photographed by Harry Stradling
and Robert Planck. Edited by Robert J. Kern. With
Norma Shearer (Consuela Croydon), Robert Taylor
(Terry Trindale), George Sanders (Tony Barling), Frank
McHugh (Chappie Champagne), Elizabeth Patterson
(Eva), Chill Wills (The Judge).

This is a film adaptation of the play Cukor directed
with Laurette Taylor. It was an unhappy experience then,
and one wonders why he returned to it. The original
production (with Jeanne Eagels replacing Miss Taylor)

ran for a hundred performances, not bad for the times, and has been a staple of summer stock ever since. (Tallulah Bankhead, who starred in it in London, often revived it on the summer circuit.) It is a highly artificial comedy concerning a young divorcee who hires a gigolo to dissuade her ex-husband from courting her again. It is a wisp of a play, with some good dialogue, and it depends upon feathery and technically assured playing if it is to pass as an enjoyable evening's entertainment.

The script fashioned from the play changes the ex-husband to an ex-suitor and makes some unfortunate excursions into bald and unfunny slapstick. Still it might have worked had it been cast correctly. *Her Cardboard Lover* demands that the actor be capable of catching every nuance of word or phrase, but with the utmost delicacy. Beyond that, he needn't do much of anything, except look elegant and move with grace. Norma Shearer lacks the technique for this kind of playing. She has all the elegance that Hollywood can buy, she strikes chic poses, but she doesn't have the timing, and she overemphasizes the lines to compensate for her inability to capture the right inflection. This kind of playing can occasionally include a wink at the audience, but Miss Shearer elbows it in the ribs. The scenes between her and Robert Taylor, who is painfully inept, are embarrassingly coy and reveal the play as the silliness it really is.

Nothing else in the film really helps matters. Only Elizabeth Patterson, a frequent contributor to Cukor's films, as the maid seems to have any idea of the style needed. The worst offender however is Cedric Gibbons's art department. The sets are fantasies weighed down by unimaginativeness. It's the kind of literal-minded whimsy that makes swans out of blocks of ice and flowers of colored icing. There isn't a clue as to where the action is supposed to be taking place. The décor suggests South

America until Chill Wills turns up as a judge and starts talking about "rights in this state," so perhaps it is meant to be California—Hollywood, probably, because where else would people live in houses inspired by Cedric Gibbons.

Keeper of the Flame (1943). Produced by Victor Saville for Metro-Goldwyn-Mayer. Script by Donald Ogden Stewart, from the novel by I. A. R. Wylie. Photographed by William Daniels. Edited by James E. Newcom. With Spencer Tracy (Steven O'Malley), Katharine Hepburn (Christine Forrest), Richard Whorf (Clive Kerndon), Margaret Wycherly (Mrs. Forrest), Frank Craven (Dr. Fielding), Horace McNally (Freddie Ridges), Percy Kilbride (Orion Peabody), Audrey Christie (Jane Harding), Darryl Hickman (Jeb Rickards), Donald Meek (Mr. Arbuthnot), Howard da Silva (Jason Rickards), William Newell (Piggot).

From the credits of *Keeper of the Flame*, one would expect it to be ideal material for Cukor. It was written by one of his frequent collaborators, it stars Katharine Hepburn and Spencer Tracy, and its supporting cast includes a large number of Broadway actors—Margaret Wycherly, Richard Whorf, who supported the Lunts several times, and Frank Craven, the original stage manager in *Our Town*.

Something, however, went wrong with the script. Mrs. Donald Ogden Stewart has said: "You know, when Don was working on *Keeper of the Flame* in 1942, Katie and Spencer Tracy went to the front office and complained. Don was bending the script to anti-fascism, and they felt as actors that something was being done to their parts."[30] Whether it was Tracy's and Hepburn's influence, or whether it was the studio's own nervousness at the possible connotations that could be read into the script, the finished film reveals some kind of interference.

The script concerns the death of a much-loved American, Robert Forrest, who leaves behind a great legend of his democracy. When a journalist begins to investigate, all sorts of barriers are placed in his way until he finally discovers that Forrest was the head of a fascist organization. Whatever political viewpoint the film has is lost in the murky atmosphere of a gothic mystery complete with a fortress-like house and a long-suffering wife. There may be some truth in the warning that behind any seemingly patriotic organization lurks the potential of treasonable activity, but the message is probed with about the same depth as those one- or two-minute shorts the British made during World War II warning that the enemy lurked everywhere. *Keeper of the Flame* has nowhere near the same cleverness.

Keeper of the Flame has that seriousness-of-purpose tone that Hollywood affects when it is sure that it is doing something worthwhile. Everybody acts as if he were at a wake, which might seem fitting for a picture that deals with a dead man, but in the long run such acting seems to imply that everyone knew he was involved with a corpse of a script.

The only redeeming factors of *Keeper of the Flame* are the glossy photography and Hepburn looking her most handsome, though she plays with that tremolo of vocal inflection she uses when uncertain of her material.

Gaslight (1944). Produced by Arthur Hornblow, Jr. for Metro-Goldwyn-Mayer. Screenplay by John van Druten, John Balderston, and Walter Reish, from the play by Patrick Hamilton. Photographed by Joseph Ruttenberg. Edited by Ralph E. Winters. With Charles Boyer (Gregory Anton), Ingrid Bergman (Paula Alquist), Joseph Cotten (Brian Cameron), Angela Lansbury (Nancy), Dame May Whitty (Miss Thwaites), Barbara Everest (Elizabeth).

Keeper of the Flame: Spencer Tracy, Katharine Hepburn
Gaslight: Charles Boyer, Ingrid Bergman

Gaslight has been one of the most successful plays of the American and English theaters.[31] It is the kind of play that still can be found in London's West End but which has almost vanished from the American stage—a psychological melodrama. It concerns the attempts of a husband to drive his wife insane for reasons that are rather complicated and not altogether convincing. Nevertheless, the play is a model of tight construction, moving with swiftness and mounting suspense to its climax.

The scriptwriters of the American version ripped the play apart at the seams. The play takes place in a period of under twelve hours; the film goes on for years and years. In fact, the film is more than half over before the first scene of the play is reached. The screenwriters have turned the original melodrama into a gothic romance of the kind that Daphne du Maurier might have written. The names and nationalities of the original characters have been changed, and the first half of the film depicts the romance of the married couple, before he starts fiddling around with the gas lamps. The film has been prettified, perhaps to satisfy the expectations of the fans of Ingrid Bergman and Charles Boyer who would expect some romantic interludes.

Ingrid Bergman can be and has been a charming actress in films such as *Casablanca, Saratoga Trunk,* and *Notorious*, but when faced with material that she believes demands her full attention as an actress, she becomes strained and serious, and her charm evaporates. This is the case in *Gaslight*. Though she gives a controlled, well-thought-out-performance, that in some of its details is even admirable, she fails to make us respond to her. Here, she lacks excitement. Charles Boyer is good in the role of the villainous husband, though he lacks the energy that overt mental cruelty requires. Joseph Cotten has the unhappy chore of playing the completely revamped character of the detective who helps the wife out of her plight. In the play, he is a roly-poly eccentric; in the film he becomes a bland second lead whose main function is to provide Miss Bergman with a happily-ever-after ending. By far the best performance in the film is given by Angela Lansbury as the pouty, provocative downstairs maid. This was Miss Lansbury's screen debut, and though she was still in her teens, she is mature in both presence and technique.

The art direction is a mixed bag. The scenes in Italy and outside the husband and wife's house in England try for a kind of Victorian picture-postcard prettiness that in execution is too literal and heavy-handed to have any charm. The London townhouse, however, is quite good; dark and cramped and crowded with bibelots, it is the kind of house that in itself could drive one mad.

Winged Victory (1944). Produced by Darryl F. Zanuck for Twentieth Century-Fox Film Corp. Screenplay by Moss Hart, from his own play. Photographed by Glen MacWilliams. Edited by Barbara McLean. With Pvt. Lon McCallister (Frankie Davis), Jeanne Crain (Helen), Sgt. Edmond O'Brien (Irving Miller), Jane Ball (Jane Preston), Sgt. Mark Daniels (Alan Ross), Jo-Carroll Dennison (Dorothy Ross), Cpl. Don Taylor (Pinky Scariano), Cpl. Lee J. Cobb (Doctor), Judy Holliday (Ruth Miller), T/Sgt. Peter Lind Hayes (O'Brian), Cpl. Alan Baxter (Major Halpert), Geraldine Wall (Mrs. Ross), Cpl. Red Buttons (Whitey), George Humbert (Mr. Scariano), Cpl. Barry Nelson (Bobby Crills), Cpl. Philip Bourneuf (Col. Gibney), Cpl. Gary Merrill (Cpt. McIntyre), Pvt. Alfred Ryder (Milhauset), Cpl. Karl Malden (Adams), Pvt. Martin Ritt (Gleason), S/Sgt. Sascha Branstoff ("Carmen Miranda"), Moyna MacGill (Mrs. Gardner), Sgt. Kevin McCarthy (Ronny Meade).

James Agee's comment on *Winged Victory* seems to me to sum it up. *"Winged Victory* has some briskly interesting and well-assembled material about the training and testing and rejecting phases of Air Force life. Aside from that I suppose it is all right, but I don't enjoy having anyone try to persuade me, so cheerfully and energetically, that the Air Force personnel is without exception composed of boy scouts old enough to shave."[32]

It is surprising that Moss Hart could not come up with something better for the wartime effort than this adenoidal drivel. It is played by a large group of men (many of whom were in the original Broadway cast in 1943) who later went on to become some of the lesser leading men of the late forties and fifties. Here, they are unbelievably callow; only Edmond O'Brien suggests that he might be capable of handling more taxing roles. The film's sole interest is that *Winged Victory* is Cukor's first meeting with Judy Holliday. Miss Holliday is the outstanding member of the cast because she brings a note of individuality to the script's homely values. She has an ordinary prettiness and a warm, sweet personality which exposes the other civilian brides who sit and wait as the cardboard figures they really are. Also good is Moyna MacGill as a scatterbrained mother. She brings the one note of true humor to a film which is overrun with frat-hazing humor and camaraderie.

Desire Me (1947). Produced by Arthur Hornblow, Jr. for Metro-Goldwyn-Mayer. Script by Zoë Akins and Marguerite Roberts from Casey Robinson's adaptation of a play and story, *Karl and Anna,* by Leonhard Frank. Photographed by Joseph Ruttenberg. Edited by Joseph Dervin. With Greer Garson (Maryse Aubert), Robert Mitchum (Paul Aubert), Richard Hart (Jean Renaud), Morris Ankrum (Martin).

Winged Victory: Don Taylor, Lon McCallister, Mark Daniels
Winged Victory: Mark Daniels, Don Taylor, Kevin McCarthy

Cukor asked that his name be removed from the credits of this film. Though he finished shooting it, later both Jack Conway and Mervyn Leroy shot some additional scenes. *Desire Me* is an uninteresting film concerning two French prisoners of war held in a German camp. One tells the other of his beautiful wife waiting at home. The second prisoner falls in love with the wife sight unseen, and when the husband is presumed to have been killed while trying to escape, he goes home to the wife. Eventually, just as the wife has fallen in love with the other man, her husband returns.

None of this makes much sense in the film, and one has to read the original play to find out what is going on. It is no surprise to discover that the play was written in the twenties (the Theatre Guild produced it in New York in 1929 with Alice Brady, Otto Kruger, and Frank Conroy in the leads), for it is one of those romantic, pessimistic plays with which post-World War I European drama abounds. These plays deal with an identity crisis that filtered through European society at the time. *Karl and Anna* is not a very good play of its kind, but the point is that the wife is so at sea in the emotional upheaval of the war that she grasps the first semblance of reality, which is the man pretending to be her husband, and learns to live with this reality so fully that when her real husband does return, she rejects him.

All of the philosophical overtones of the play have been totally erased in the screenplay; to satisfy the Hays Office, the script also had to be altered because the original play obviously dealt with adultery. The one thing that hasn't been erased is the unmistakable feeling that the over-all atmosphere of the film belongs to an earlier era. In every way, *Desire Me* is out of joint.

As in *A Woman's Face*, the film begs for trouble by using American and English actors as European peasants.

Robert Mitchum as a Breton fisherman is an absurd piece of casting. This was Richard Hart's screen debut after a success on the stage the previous season in *Dark of the Moon*, and though he is a competent actor, he does not convey the excitement that one should feel for a new face entrusted with a major role. Greer Garson, who had been momentarily charming in *Goodbye, Mr. Chips*, was still playing Mrs. Miniver, and such decorum and gentility become overwhelming handicaps.

Edward, My Son (1948). Produced by Edwin H. Knopf for Metro-Goldwyn-Mayer. Script by Donald Ogden Stewart, from the play by Robert Morley and Noel Langley. Photographed by Frederick A. Young. Edited by Raymond Poulton. With Spencer Tracy (Arnold Boult), Deborah Kerr (Evelyn Boult), Ian Hunter (Doctor Larry Woodhope), James Donald (Bronton), Mervyn Johns (Harry Simpkins), Leueen McGrath (Eileen Perrin), Walter Fitzgerald (M. Kedner).

Edward, My Son is one of those earnestly intelligent but basically mundane exercises in the drama which the British theater at its most mediocre produces. It is a study of a self-made man who ruthlessly destroys anyone and anything that threatens his totally worthless son. The play consciously sets out to capture the sounds and manners of a certain stratum of life and artfully arranges them into a pattern of drama, without noticing that the basic premise springs not from life but from literary cliches. Given the bare outline of the plot of *Edward, My Son,* one can guess the details: the wife driven to drink; the mistress who loves in spite of herself and smiles knowingly throughout, for she realizes her end is in her beginning; the little shop-girl whom the son impregnates, and whom dad tries to buy off, etc. Still, it is done with taste, and it is polished by highly literate dialogue that in the past guaranteed success with a certain audience. *Edward, My Son* also has a dash of theatricality: the father, at the beginning and the end of the play, speaks directly to the audience, asking them to judge him. It is just the right amount of daring acceptable to the theater audience for whom the play is geared.

As the father Robert Morley, the co-author, had great success both in London and New York. But he probably wasn't considered an important enough name to be entrusted with the role on the screen, which went to Spencer Tracy. The screenplay makes one attempt to alter the character of the father to fit Tracy—he becomes a Canadian immigrant, thus eliminating the need for the actor to attempt an accent. In the opening scenes of the play, the father is likeable, and throughout the play he exhibits a veneer of charm that initially fools people as to his ruthless personality. Morley can be a likeable actor, but he has an element of the sinister, too, probably because of his huge frame and his small, piercing eyes. Tracy's screen image, however, is one of extreme amiability; through his roles a friendly man always shines through, gruff at times but never unpleasant. The role in *Edward, My Son* doesn't fit Tracy, and he doesn't seem at home in it. His own personality, reinforced by the audience's knowledge of past roles, stubbornly refuses to coincide with the character.

Edward, My Son, made at MGM's English studios, was Cukor's first film outside the United States. With the exception of Tracy, the rest of the cast is by and large British, and they give the film that feeling of solidity that English supporting players, even when they are only average, lend to a film. Leueen McGrath made a name for herself in the part of the mistress (she created it on the stage), but she gives the part a note of smugness. As the alcoholic, long-suffering wife, Deborah Kerr gives a harrowing performance which alternates between inner rage and self-pity. Her voice has an overly emotional timbre, but she plays against it, holds it in check, and by doing so creates an arresting tension. She works carefully; the performance is skillfully built and delicately shaded. The final effect, however, is almost flamboyant because the emotion she has planned is so huge and so fully supported. Miss Kerr's performance ranks as one of the finest pieces of acting in Cukor's films.

Edward, My Son: Deborah Kerr, Spencer Tracy

Born Yesterday: Broderick Crawford, Judy Holliday

Gordon and Kanin, Solo and in Tandem

Ruth Gordon and Garson Kanin were married in 1942. Miss Gordon was already one of America's foremost actresses. Garson Kanin had had a checkered career as a saxophonist, clarinetist, actor, and stage and film director, gaining fame in the latter category. After their marriage, both the Kanins added writing to their many other activities.

The collaborative writing efforts of the Kanins have been restricted to film. Beginning in 1947, with *A Double Life*, they wrote four screenplays and asked George Cukor, who had directed Miss Gordon in *Two-Faced Woman*, to direct them. In addition, each one wrote a single screenplay for Cukor. Indeed, one can say that the years between 1947 and 1954 in Cukor's activity are dominated by the Kanins, and their efforts enabled Cukor to rise above the slump his career had been suffering since the early forties.

Cukor has said of his collaboration with the Kanins:

It was a very harmonious thing. It's unique because Garson was a very experienced director. Very often people would say, "Oh, didn't you do that well!" and I'd say, "I hate to admit it, but that was written in the script." Garson would say, "Don't move the camera" or "Do move the camera" or something. Often they were already in the script. He did it. And maybe we just worked on the same beam. I have a regard for him. Often we'd have ad libs we'd have to do. I haven't a gift for writing, so I would call Ruth and Garson in New York and say, "Look, we need some ad lib" or even "What do I do about that line" or "This was just so-so" and they'd say, "Just a moment . . . we'll call you back in half an hour." And they would and they'd have the correction. I have great regard for their knowledge and maybe that's because I came from the theater as they do.[33]

Whatever their failings might be, the Kanins' scripts had a New Yorkish sophistication and a literate polish that encouraged Cukor's whole-hearted participation. The Kanins also wrote their screenplays especially for actors whom Cukor enjoyed directing—Katharine Hepburn, Spencer Tracy, and Judy Holliday. The enjoyment that the actors and director had in working together gives these films an elusive but nonetheless tangible warmth.

A Double Life (1947). Produced by Michael Kanin for Universal-International. Script by Ruth Gordon and Garson Kanin. Photographed by Milton Krasner. Edited by Robert Parrish. *Othello* scenes staged by Walter Hampden. With Ronald Colman (Tony John), Signe Hasso (Brita Kaurin), Edmond O'Brien (Bill Friend), Shelley Winters (Pat Kroll), Philip Loeb (Max Lasker), Ray Collins (Victor), Millard Mitchell (Al Cooley), John Drew Colt (Stage Manager), Whit Bissell (Dr. Stauffer), Fay Kanin and Frederic Worlock (in *Othello* scenes), Elliott Reid (in *A Gentlemen's Gentleman* scenes), Betsy Blair (Girl in Wig Shop).

Cukor and the Kanins collaborated on comedies with one exception, *A Double Life*. Nevertheless its show-business milieu links it to their other works, singly and as a team. The show-biz story falls into three general categories. First, the bitchy comedy (*All About Eve*); then, the "waiting in the wings for the big break" musical (such as *Golddiggers*); and finally, "the horror that lurks beneath the applause" drama (*A Star Is Born, Sunset Boulevard, The Bad and the Beautiful*). *A Double Life* belongs to the last category, since it deals with an actor who, while playing Othello, finds the Moor's jealousy invading his private life.

The subject, based upon a documented professional hazard, is potentially intriguing. But however realistic it may be, it is still a singularly romantic idea. The same theme has been handled brilliantly in Marcel Carné's *Les*

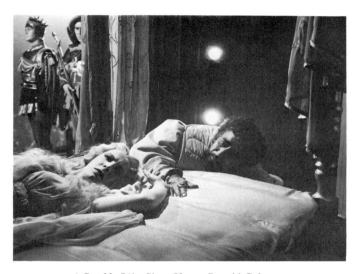

A Double Life: Signe Hasso, Ronald Colman
Adam's Rib: Spencer Tracy, Katharine Hepburn

Enfants du paradis, in which one of the leading characters, Frédérick Lemaître, suffers the identical problem while playing the same role. Carné's film has the poetic intensity, the hot-house elegance, the heightened sensibility and emotion that are the hallmarks of the romantic temperament. But *A Double Life* falls back on that insistent purple-prose treatment journalists use when faced with an extremely bizarre murder case. Within the setting of Milton Krasner's chiaroscuro photography, Miklas Rosza's insistently "symphonic" score, and the portentous acting, writing, and directing, this theatrical murder shrivels into insignificant shoptalk.

The film's possibilities are also hampered by Ronald Colman's performance as Tony John, the jealous actor. At the time of the film's release, this role was widely considered the best that Colman had received during his long career, a career based largely upon his ability to play cardboard lovers with dependable charm. His main distinctions as an actor were his aristocratic looks and mellifluous voice. He was, however, uninspired, and he had polished his competence into a polished competence. His performance lacks the theatrical daring and the passion needed to touch our imagination.

Most of the Kanin films are set in New York, and they were filmed, in part, on location. There's nothing wrong with Cukor's location work in these films, but it lacks a genuinely sensual response. In the Cukor-Kanin films, location work makes a very real contribution to the actuality of the stories, and one is not jolted, as one is by the Greenwich Village sequences in Cukor's *Let's Make Love*, by the artificiality of studio work. The theater scenes which play an integral part in *A Double Life* were shot in that most historic and elegant of New York theaters, the Empire, which was criminally torn down in 1953.

Adam's Rib (1949). Produced by Lawrence Weingarten for Metro-Goldwyn-Mayer. Script by Ruth Gordon and Garson Kanin. Photographed by George J. Folsey. Edited by George Boemler. "Farewell, Amanda" by Cole Porter. With Katharine Hepburn (Amanda Bonner), Spencer Tracy (Adam Bonner), Judy Holliday (Doris Attinger), Tom Ewell (Warren Attinger), David Wayne (Kip Lurie), Jean Hagen (Beryl Caighn), Hope Emerson (Olympia), Eve March (Grace), Clarence Kolb (Judge Reisner), Polly Moran (Mrs. McGrath).

This is a smart and sassy comedy and a great favorite of many people. I'm afraid, however, that it is a little too coy for my taste. I wish the husband and wife characters played by Mr. Tracy and Miss Hepburn didn't call each other "Pinky"; I wish they didn't show such cutesy home movies; I wish that during a trial scene Hope Emerson didn't lift Tracy off the ground with the heft of one hand; I would prefer if neither Tracy nor Hepburn played with such intense archness. Most of all I wish that suddenly halfway through the film Judy Holliday, Tom Ewell, and Jean Hagen did not momentarily change sexes right before our eyes. In a flash all the good will we have worked up goes down the drain, and we cringe in our seats. The Kanins have a predilection for this kind of imaginary or dream sequence—there's one in *The Marrying Kind* and in *Pat and Mike* also—but they haven't the flair to carry them off. The prosaic writing and a literal-mindedness in Cukor's staging keep them painfully earthbound.

Still, all in all, *Adam's Rib* is an enjoyable film. There are any number of bright lines as well as great polish in the staging. The supporting cast is uniformly excellent. Judy Holliday, returning to film after her success on stage in *Born Yesterday*, is both comic and touching. At this time, Miss Holliday was fighting for the part of Billie Dawn in the film version of *Born Yesterday*, and Cukor gave her the opportunity to showcase her talents. Her first scene with Katharine Hepburn is done in one long take (a sure sign that Cukor likes and trusts an actor), and it favors Miss Holliday throughout. David Wayne is also very appealing as the composer who is a neighbor of Tracy's and Hepburn's. Wayne's puckishness is judiciously handled so that it never becomes overbearingly fey as it does in some films.

There are two side attractions in the film: "Farewell, Amanda," one of Cole Porter's most inconsequential but still catchy, lightly sardonic songs (written while he was on a cruise, it was originally called "Bye Bye Samoa"), and a flowery, beribboned bonnet which Tracy gives Hepburn and which she later passes on to Miss Holliday. It has the comic sweetness that the rest of the film tries for but often misses by overreaching.

Born Yesterday (1950). Produced by S. Sylvan Simon for Columbia Pictures Corp. Script by Albert Mannheimer from the play by Garson Kanin. Photographed by Joseph Walker. Edited by Charles Nelson. With Judy Holliday (Billie Dawn), Broderick Crawford (Harry Brock), William Holden (Paul Verrall), Howard St. John (Jim Devery), Frank Otto (Eddie), Larry Oliver (Norval Hedges), Barbara Brown (Mrs. Hedges), Grandon Rhodes (Sanborn), Claire Carleton (Helen).

Judy Holliday won the part of Billie Dawn against the wishes of Harry Cohn, the head of Columbia Pictures, who couldn't envision her as a movie star. To help him do so, the make-up department of Columbia tried to glamorize her by doing her hair à la Harpo Marx, overpainting her face, and putting her in a number of unbecoming dresses by Jean Louis.

Happily, Miss Holliday manages to overcome these obstacles. Her primary gift as an actress was her ability to deliver the lines as though they had just come into her head. Cukor has said:

Judy Holliday would speak not only every "if," "and," and "but," but she'd speak the punctuation marks. If Garson Kanin had a question mark, she'd read it like a question; and yet, you had the sense that she'd made that up as she went along—she knew how to do it.[34]

At certain points in *Born Yesterday* her timing, which was generally excellent, seems a shade off. This may be due to the fact that she had played the part so many times on the stage that her rhythms are still geared that way. For instance, the famous line, "You wanna wash your hands or anything, honey?" is off a beat, and there is too long a pause following it, waiting for a laugh that doesn't build as strongly as suspected. This is partially Cukor's fault, for this is one of his least successful adaptations of plays. The camera placements are not always judicious—often they move into the action too closely. Frequently the film is as boring to watch as a TV show, for it is in large part a succession of medium shots and close-ups.

Because of financial disagreements with Columbia, Kanin did not do his own adaptation of the script, although, according to Cukor, he did outline it for Albert Mannheimer, who followed the play faithfully. He has cleaned up some of the dirtier lines and rearranged the one-set, three-act structure to include many settings (most of them historic Washington monuments), but practically all of the action and dialogue is Kanin's. *Born Yesterday* had a weak final act that was overcome by the strength of the rest of the play. Cukor was aware of this, and it is one of the examples he cites of filming weaknesses as well as strengths in order not to lose the vitality of the original. This sounds good, but it really evades the issue. There really is no third act other than the one Kanin wrote.

Given the idea of a dumb Dora of a showgirl who bones up on politics, there is no other way to end it than by having her give everyone else lessons in democracy. The inherent problem is that Billie is lots of fun when she's dumb, but after a course in seventh-grade civics, she's a drag, and she drags the play down with her as she "oohs" and "aahs" over the Bill of Rights and the architecture of the Jefferson Memorial.

The film in some ways makes this ending more palatable because of the casting. William Holden's innate likeability tones down a lot of the priggishness of the character of the writer, and makes him charming; whereas the role of Harry Brock, which was played on the stage with a mixture of violence and charm by Paul Douglas, on screen becomes disagreeable because of Broderick Crawford's presence. The casting of Crawford may have been forced on Cukor by the studio, since Harry Cohn had already given in on Judy Holliday. Crawford plays the role as a typical heavy in a Grade B melodrama. Like the character of Harry Brock, Crawford lacks a sense of humor, but the actor to play the role has to have what the character lacks. There is no sense of fun in Crawford's playing, no charm. He is as Brock might have been were he a person in real life rather than a theatrical character. His performance saps the film of much of the humor that was the source of the play's vitality.

The Marrying Kind (1951). Produced by Bert Granet for Columbia Pictures Corp. Script by Ruth Gordon and Garson Kanin. Photographed by Joseph Walker. Edited by Charles Nelson. With Judy Holliday (Florence Keefer), Aldo Ray (Chet Keefer), Madge Kennedy (Judge Carroll), Sheila Bond (Joan Shipley), John Alexander (Howard Shipley), Rex Williams (George Bastian), Phyllis Povah (Mrs. Derringer), Peggy Cass (Emily

Born Yesterday: Judy Holliday, Broderick Crawford
The Marrying Kind: Judy Holliday, Aldo Ray

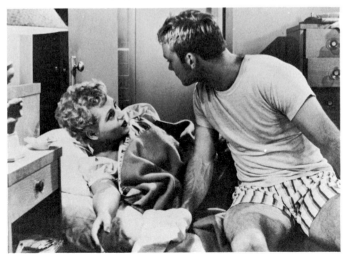

Bundy), Mickey Shaunessy (Pat Bundy), Griff Barnett (Charley), Susan Hallaren (Ellen), Christie Olsen (Joey), Barry Curtis (Joey at an older age), Wallace Actorn (Newhouse), Elsie Holmes (Marian).

The Marrying Kind is one of those films in which Hollywood occasionally casts its eye on the "little" people of this earth, the John and Jane Does of America. Florence and Chet Keefer are getting a divorce; a kind-hearted lady judge who thinks they are making a mistake gets them to talk about their marriage. Much of the humor of the film comes from the fact that as one member of the ménage tells his story, the other member visualizes an entirely different version.

The script avoids the excesses of TV situation comedy though that's really where its heart lies. The study of Stuyvesant Town marriage goes through all the middle-class cliché situations concerning newlyweds. There is always the suspicion that the authors haven't the remotest knowledge of what they are writing about, and that their model is not real life but what they have read in magazines and newspapers and seen in the movies. Yet the authors write with a deftness and geniality that quiet our strongest objections. Then, too, Cukor and his cast bring to the film a warmth that is winning. They also manage to blend with skill the comic and the pathetic moments of the film into a unified whole.

Miss Holliday was an expert at this kind of thing. She was one of those funny girls who, with a twitch of a face muscle, could break your heart. Her appeal was not calculated but was quite genuine; one feels as if one were responding to a real person.

Aldo Ray has some of this same quality, and he is more likeable here than he has been since, but an actor less like Miss Holliday would have increased the film's comic tension. The rest of the cast is almost entirely composed of New York actors, which gives texture and credibility to the film's background, as does the location shooting. Most notable among these players is Madge Kennedy as the judge. Several of the other actors, though they look right, play much too broadly. When Sheila Bond or Mickey Shaunessy or Peggy Cass are on the screen, the whole thing begins to look suspiciously like *I Love Lucy*.

Pat and Mike (1952). Produced by Lawrence Weingarten for Metro-Goldwyn-Mayer. Screenplay by Ruth Gordon and Garson Kanin. Photographed by William Daniels. Edited by George Boemler. With Katharine Hepburn (Pat Pemberton), Spencer Tracy (Mike Conovan), Aldo Ray (Davie Hucko), William Ching (Collier Weld), Sammy White (Barney Gran), Phyllis Povah (Mrs. Beminger), Loring Smith (Mr. Beminger), Chuck Connors (Police Captain). And Gussie Moran, Babe Didrikson Zaharias, Don Budge, Alice Marble, Frank Parker, Betty Hicks, Beverly Hanson, Helen Dettweiler as themselves.

Pat and Mike pleases because of modest intentions and fresh execution. It hasn't much plot, and its dialogue isn't as smart as that written by Gordon and Kanin for *Adam's Rib*, but it doesn't fight as hard for laughs.

Hepburn and Tracy, playing together for the seventh time, have polished their interplay to give the impression of a relaxed, amusing game. As they volley effortlessly the jibes and endearments of the script, they exhibit such warmth and enjoyment that the audience can bask in it. There is none of the mugging or archness that marred their playing in *Adam's Rib*.

Pat and Mike is built around Hepburn's abilities as a sportswoman, and she goes through her athletic paces with zest and grace. Much of the enjoyment of the film comes from watching her during these scenes. At one point, Tracy says of the character played by Hepburn,

"There's not much meat on her, but what's there is cherce." It may be the definitive comment on Hepburn.

It is also the biggest laugh in the film, and part of the reason it is so funny is because it isn't stressed. *Pat and Mike* is rather freely shot, not always following the Hollywood lexicon of how things should be done. There is also freedom in the use of the sound track—there is a lot of overlapping dialogue. Cukor remembers shooting the scene that includes Tracy's big laugh:

One of the great big laughs—now mind you, you've got to know who's speaking the line and how good the laugh is—one of the big laughs of the thing, "There's not much meat on her, but what's there is cherce," was spoken by Spencer Tracy in an almost full figure shot. He was turned almost three-quarters away from the audience. We didn't cut to a close-up for emphasis—Tracy is such a strong actor. I didn't even shoot a close-up for protection in case we found we needed it later. Somehow, we had courage, and we shot it just the way it is seen, just let it go and said, "Well, if it's good, it's good. . . ."

Afterwards, Tracy was very amusing about it. When people would say, "Oh, you were just great in it," he'd say, "I was just as great in the last picture, but I didn't get a laugh at all. It must have something to do with the material." He gave due credit to the situation the Kanins had created.[35]

The Actress (1953). Produced by Lawrence Weingarten for Metro-Goldwyn-Mayer. Script by Ruth Gordon, from her play *Years Ago*. Photographed by Harold Rosson. Edited by George Boemler. With Spencer Tracy (Clinton Jones), Jean Simmons (Ruth Jones), Teresa Wright (Mrs. Jones), Anthony Perkins (Fred Whitmarsh), Ian Wolfe (Mr. Bagley), Kay Williams (Hazel Dawn), Mary Wickes (Gym Instructress).

Upon its release in 1953, *The Actress* was moderately successful, as had been Miss Gordon's autobiographical play, *Years Ago*, upon which it is based. *The Actress* is an appealing film; it is that rarity—a nice film.

The adjective "nice" carries the connotation of something that's not very exciting, and that, too, is true of *The Actress*. It's a film that's so busy with being sweet and gentle and folksy, so concerned with having us nod and smile at it, that it almost lulls us to sleep. Partially, this is because of the acting. Teresa Wright as the mother acts with such quiet understatedness that she almost wipes herself off the screen. Anthony Perkins in his first screen role is the epitome of the vapid juvenile. As Ruth (Gordon) Jones, Jean Simmons makes some impression because she is an excellent, secure actress. What is missing from her performance here, and this is probably inherent in the writing of the role and the way it must be played, is the ability to make us believe that this girl has any talent for the stage. Nothing she does in the film convinces us that she is more than a moony, stage-struck kid. Simmons gives a recitation during the film which is meant to prove to her father that she should go on the stage. When it is over there is nothing for us to do but share her father's opinion that she should become a physical education teacher. From the way the scene is written it is clear that the girl is meant to make no impression on the father and probably she should be terrible. It should, however, be terribleness with a difference. Katharine Hepburn achieved this in a similar moment in *Morning Glory* when she recited a soliloquy from *Hamlet*. Awful as it was, one could feel, as did the other characters in the film, that there was something special and striking about this girl which, if mined, might make her an actress.

The fault lies in the writing. What Miss Gordon has failed to include in her autobiography is her own character. Perhaps she wanted to write about all actresses, but like many authors who try for universality of theme, she has mistakenly stripped the character of any individuality, which is the one thing that might make her story pertinent to us. In the film the portrait of the girl was further weakened by insensitive cutting that upset both Miss Gordon and Cukor.

The title, *The Actress*, is a misnomer anyway, because the play and the film are really about the actress's father, a gruff, salty New Englander with (yes) a heart of gold. Spencer Tracy's performance has drawn raves, but his "naturalistic" underplaying here becomes the worst kind of mugging.[36] Cukor, who greatly admired Tracy, compounds the error by favoring him in practically every shot. Still, Tracy gives the only real vitality to the film, and he does have at least one scene in which he is admirable: he talks about his youth with an understated vehemence that is rather startling within the context of the scene.

Another very nice scene shows Miss Simmons watching, from the upper balcony of a Boston theater, an early-twentieth-century musical, *The Pink Lady* (1911). Onstage is Hazel Dawn, the show's star, singing her great hit, the waltz "My Beautiful Lady." Kay Williams, who plays Hazel Dawn, was, like Madge Kennedy in *The Marrying Kind*, a popular stage star of that same period in which Cukor and Ruth Gordon entered the theater professionally. Cukor has re-created these scenes from the kind of theater he watched as a stage-struck kid with great affection and with enough fidelity to suggest the charm of old stage photographs.

One thing that the Gordon-Kanin scripts proved was that Cukor, who during the thirties worked mainly with rather elegant café-society backgrounds, could respond to stories that dealt with more homely people and settings. In particular, these films are reserved and realistic (if

The Actress: Jean Simmons
It Should Happen to You: Jack Lemmon, Judy Holliday

never inspired) in art direction. One of the nicest things about *The Actress* is the setting for the home in which the actress and her family live. Before the film began production, Cukor and Miss Gordon paid a visit to her family's home in Walliston, Massachusetts; Miss Gordon was shocked at how small it was. The house as re-created for the film is marvelously cramped and dark, with the spirit of New England Puritanism hovering in its atmosphere.[37]

It Should Happen to You (1953). Produced by Fred Kohlmar for Columbia Pictures Corp. Script by Garson Kanin. Photographed by Charles Lang. Edited by Charles Nelson. With Judy Holliday (Gladys Glover), Jack Lemmon (Peter Sheppard), Peter Lawford (Evan Adams), Michael O'Shea (Brod Clinton), Vaughn Taylor (Entrikin), Connie Gilchrist (Mrs. Riker), Walter Kalvun (Bert Piazza), Melville Cooper (Guest on TV panel show). And Wendy Barrie, Constance Bennett, Ilka Chase as themselves.

Of all the films Cukor made with one or both of the Kanins, this is my favorite, if only because of the delightful performances of Judy Holliday and Jack Lemmon. The script itself doesn't fulfill its promise. It concerns a girl who wants to be famous (the original, much better, title of the film was *A Name for Herself*) and places her name on a huge billboard on the pre-Coliseum Columbus Circle. Soon the girl finds herself an overnight celebrity on TV panel shows. Eventually it dawns on her that she has become some kind of freak, and she gives up her fame for marriage to a documentary film-maker.

It Should Happen to You would be better for sharper satire of the kind Ben Hecht provided in his earlier study of a freak celebrity, Hazel Flagg, in *Nothing Sacred*. Kanin and Cukor are much too genial for that kind of acerbic humor, and their treatment of the advertising and TV industries comes out as a kind of good-natured lampoon. It's satire without any teeth in its bite.

The character of Gladys Glover is one of those kind-hearted, upright, almost simple-minded characters with which Miss Holliday was saddled throughout her career, but the part was written for her, and Kanin obviously counted on the qualities that she would bring to it. Miss Holliday is intrinsically so sympathetic and plays with such infectious delight that one can't help responding.

Jack Lemmon gives what is perhaps his most appealing performance in film. Though Cukor evidently had some problems getting Lemmon to scale down his performance for this, his first screen role, he seems a born film actor. There is a freshness and naturalness here that he would later exploit. He is an excellent foil for Miss Holliday. His down-to-earthness is an effective counterpoint for her whimsy. Even their ways of getting angry complement each other: her rather self-righteous huffiness versus his explosive stammering rage. *The Marrying Kind* could have been a more effective film had Lemmon and not Aldo Ray played the husband. Cukor also gave a new direction to Peter Lawford's career by casting him in the role of the advertising executive. Lawford had passed his prime as a suave juvenile, and Cukor used the suavity as a kind of oiliness that guaranteed the actor a new career in character roles.

Quite the most charming moment in this film is when Miss Holliday and Lemmon sing Harold Arlen's "Let's Fall in Love," originally written for a 1934 Columbia film of the same title. It is a relaxed, lazy song, and the singers give it an impromptu, amateurish quality that is altogether winning. This scene epitomizes what makes the best Cukor-Gordon-Kanin films appealing: there is a modesty about their intentions and something so good-natured about their realization that they are disarming.

A Star Is Born: Judy Garland

The Musicals

Cukor began directing musicals at the very time that the form was dying out in Hollywood. The last great screen musical, the greatest of them all, was *Singin' in the Rain* in 1952. Since then, there have been mainly the blockbusters, based on Broadway hits. Whatever had caused the blooming of musical talent in Hollywood in the late forties died on the bough, and most of the original musicals of the fifties and early sixties reverted to the oldest form of the song-and-dance film—the backstage story. In this format, song and dance don't advance the plot but serve as interludes that depict a show that is being put on within the movie. Three of Cukor's four musicals fall into this category; the remaining, *My Fair Lady*, is, of course, one of the blockbuster adaptations of Broadway shows.

The musical changed after the forties; it became too serious. It lost most of what is appealing in the form—its connections with vaudeville, music hall, and burlesque—and retained what was worst—the link with the operetta. (The musical has never recovered from the blow given it by the "Soliloquy" in Rodgers and Hammerstein's *Carousel*.) Song and dance were saddled with making points that were too serious or alien for the popular song to encompass. Non-singers and dancers had to be cast in the leading roles, because the book was too demanding to be left in the hands of anyone other than serious actors. With no songs to sing and no one to sing them, the form began to die.

The problem became worse in Hollywood as the age of specialization died. There was a time when the studios were geared to turn out so many comedies, so many women's pictures, so many mysteries, and so many musicals a year, and the studio kept a stable of experts for each category. When the era of the long-term-contract employee ended, so did specialization. Ironically, the musical specialists turned to other kinds of film (without much success) and non-musical directors turned (with even less success) to the musical.

Cukor entered the musical in this period, and his work reflects the problems of the musical at this time. Often his musical collaborators are not the best. Rarely are the musical numbers smoothly integrated into the rest of the film. There is the feeling that these are films with musical numbers included for those who dote on the form, but with enough other values to intrigue those who hate it.

A Star Is Born (1954). Produced by Sid Luft for Warner Bros. Pictures, Inc. Script by Moss Hart, from an original screenplay by Dorothy Parker, Alan Campbell, and Robert Carson. Photographed by Sam Leavitt. Edited by Folmar Blangsted. Color consultation by George Hoyningen-Huene. Music by Harold Arlen. Lyrics by Ira Gershwin. "Born in a Trunk" written by Leonard Gershe, music by Roger Edens, choreography by Richard Barstow. Other choreography by Eugene Loring. With Judy Garland (Esther Blodgett, Vicky Lester), James Mason (Norman Maine), Jack Carson (Matt Libby), Charles Bickford (Oliver Niles), Tommy Noonan (Danny McGuire), Lucy Marlow (Lola Lavery), Amanda Blake (Susan), Irving Bacon (Graves).

This is a film of which Cukor seems particularly fond and one that is greatly loved by many people, but it is very uneven. The first problem is that the script does not give itself to updating. The Hollywood it depicts is the Hollywood of the thirties. By the mid-fifties the film industry had already begun its decline; stars weren't being born (except on TV), and the few that were born weren't musical stars. The depiction of an Academy Award presentation is an anachronism; in this film it is a relatively small, family affair held in a restaurant (as these presentations

A Star Is Born: James Mason, Judy Garland

were in the early years) rather than the TV spectacular this event has been since the early fifties. The film never pinpoints dates, so perhaps it is supposed to be taking place in the thirties. The sets and costumes, however, do not give this impression, but then Hollywood in the fifties had a tendency to present the past in present-day dress. Perhaps this film uses this terribly confusing convention.

A Star Is Born is really a straight script; the musical numbers don't make plot points, they expand them. Cukor has said:

The picture was, in fact, too long. But while I wasn't there they produced a big production number right in the middle—"Born in a Trunk." It went on and on and in the context of the final cut version was way too long. If they thought it was too long there were other ways of shortening it besides chopping and hacking out vital bits. Had we been allowed, Moss Hart and I could have sweated out twenty minutes which would have been imperceptible to the audience.[38]

Warner's had cut the major portions of two musical numbers, "Lose that Long Face" and "Here's What I'm Here For," neither of them very good, and a number of short scenes early in the film about what happened to Vicky Lester from the time she first meets Norman Maine to their second encounter after he has returned from location shooting. The film is much smoother dramatically with these scenes, and they also help Garland's performance because in them she is lighter and easier than she is in most other moments of the film.

The additional and justifiably famous "Born in a Trunk" sequence is indeed totally extraneous to the film. But then so are all the other songs. By far the best is "The Man That Got Away," sung by Garland in what appears to be one monumental take (probably shot with two or three cameras). Visually it is a most striking sequence, with extremely mobile camera movement that seems to catch the action off the cuff. Garland sings the torch song with all her considerable emotional savvy. Later in the film the show is stopped again by Garland's impromptu production number, "Somewhere There's a Someone," staged to get Norman out of the dumps. Again, Garland and the staging and the camera work are all absolutely stunning, but they just aren't integrated into the texture of the story. The songs are all overproduced, using the same kind of oversell that unsure Broadway musicals now use to razzle-dazzle their audiences.

A Star Is Born is a very handsome musical. Although Cukor does not like the shape of the CinemaScope screen, he uses it imaginatively. He has said that his use of the new format was inspired by the fragments of paintings reproduced in art books:

You're used to seeing the whole of a thing—then suddenly you see a section, arbitrarily, not composed. . . . And I thought why not do that in a movie? We made use of this especially when Judy Garland sang "The Man that Got Away." In a little night club after hours the camera followed her always in front . . . sometimes she went to the side and almost disappeared out of the frame . . . she was rarely right in the middle.[39]

A Star Is Born was the first film to use the wide screen with fluidity and imagination and to recapture the sense of intimacy that the first of the 'Scope films had lost.

A great deal of the imagination and taste exhibited in Cukor's color films is the result of his collaboration with George Hoyningen-Huene. The two have worked together on all of Cukor's color films except *My Fair Lady* and *Justine.* Hoyningen-Huene was a distinguished fashion photographer for *Vogue, Harper's Bazaar,* and *Flair.* In Cukor's films he coordinated the color in the sets, costumes, and photography. The color is usually highly stylized, often depending upon splashes of one primary color set off by one, two, rarely more than three, muted shades. It is very simple, but it gives an effect of dazzling but tasteful elegance.

The film is exceedingly well acted. Jack Carson's performance as Libby, the dyspeptic, T. S. Eliot-quoting press agent, is the best of the actor's career. Charles Bickford manages to make a presence out of the essentially bland character of Oliver Niles, the head of the studio. By far the best performance is given by James Mason as Norman Maine. It is a difficult task to play a drunk without asking for pity or becoming gross, but Mason is an actor of tact and sensitivity, and he makes Norman a charming and humorous man, a genuinely attractive and good person. He is the most likable of all the many sympathetically drawn drunks in Cukor's films. Cukor's sympathy toward alcoholics may stem from his friendship with John Barrymore, but it is, more importantly, symptomatic of the director's unwillingness to judge his characters because of their weaknesses.

Cukor has said many times that Judy Garland's performance here reminds him of the quality of Laurette Taylor. Garland has the daring openness of emotion, the wounded vulnerability, the charm and warmth with which Laurette Taylor was said to captivate her audience. Garland's Vicky Lester is a striking performance, and one cannot remain unaffected by it. It is brave and honest and true, and it is played with nerve ends exposed.

Nonetheless, it is wrong for the character. Vicky Lester marries Norman Maine, a has-been alcoholic actor, because she believes that her love will give him new strength. Vicky has to be fresh, healthy, and strong. From the outset, Garland's performance is so naked that one is struck immediately by a powerful neurosis at work. Garland brought to the role personal qualities that she could not strip from herself as an actress, and I think that this is what a great number of her fans are responding to. Cukor was perhaps so overwhelmed by the openness and hugeness of emotion of Garland's performance—and it is impressive—that he miscalculated the emphasis it would give the role.

Les Girls (1957). Produced by Sol C. Siegel for Metro-Goldwyn-Mayer. Script by John Patrick, from a story by Vera Caspary. Photographed by Robert Surtees. Edited by Ferris Webster. Color consultation by George Hoyningen-Huene. Choreography by Jack Cole. Music and lyrics by Cole Porter. With Gene Kelly (Barry Nichols), Kay Kendall (Lady Sibyl Wren), Mitzi Gaynor (Joy Henderson), Taina Elg (Angele Duclos), Jacques Bergerac (Pierre Duclos), Leslie Phillips (Sir Gerald Wren), Henry Daniell (Judge).

Les Girls also uses the backstage story. This time it concerns a former showgirl who writes her memoirs and is promptly sued for slander by another girl in the troupe. In court we hear (and are shown) three different versions of "the truth."

Elegant production values help cover the pale wit of John Patrick's script. The film is never as smart as it wants to be, but the color (as it is in all of the films Cukor made with Hoyningen-Huene) is terribly chic, and through a limited number of sets (most of them, wisely, interiors), the art direction does create a credible musical-comedyish Paris, London, and Madrid.

Cole Porter's songs are not his best,[40] and the staging is worse. Choreographer Jack Cole's combination of neo-native, sub-Martha Graham dance patterns is the nadir of the American musical's flirtation with "culture," and it is nowhere better exemplified than the number in which

Gene Kelly is wrapped up in a lot of nylon cord by a predatory Taina Elg; it is an unintentional burlesque of Jerome Robbins's *The Cage*, done against sets that are like a dreadful take-off of Isamu Noguchi's set designs for Martha Graham.

In the acting department, a note of distinction comes from Kay Kendall, one of those rare women who is truly beautiful and truly comic (and in her physical make-up the beauty and the comic go hand-in-hand, for her incredible ski-jump nose gives her loveliness the peculiarity that distinctive beauty needs). It is only when Miss Kendall gives her drunken rendition of "La Habanera" that the film goes into high gear. Taina Elg, though she is unattractively made-up, is also appealing as the second of "Les Girls," but Mitzi Gaynor as the third of the trio has that indigestible wholesomeness that only in the fifties would guarantee her the role of the girl who gets the man.

Let's Make Love (1960). Produced by Jerry Wald for Twentieth Century-Fox Film Corp. Script by Norman Krasna. Photographed by Daniel L. Fapp. Color consultation by George Hoyningen-Huene. Edited by Daniel Bretherton. Songs by Cole Porter, Jimmy Van Heusen, and Sammy Cahn. With Marilyn Monroe (Amanda Pell), Yves Montand (Jean-Marc Clement), Tony Randall (Howard Coffman), Frankie Vaughan (Tony Danton), Wilfrid Hyde-White (John Whales), David Burns (Oliver Burton). And Milton Berle, Gene Kelly, and Bing Crosby as themselves.

Let's Make Love ranks with *Desire Me, Zaza*, and *A Life of Her Own* in Cukor's quartet of worst films. Norman Krasna, who wrote this film, is an immensely successful Broadway and Hollywood writer, specializing in a certain kind of fabricated comedy. *Let's Make Love* concerns a billionaire who joins an off-Broadway revue

Les Girls: Taina Elg, Kay Kendall, Mitzi Gaynor
Let's Make Love: Marilyn Monroe, Yves Montand

and learns to sing, dance, and tell funny stories in order to hear the leading lady say "I love you" to him instead of his billions. We are again in the realm of the backstage musical, this time in its purest form, for not one of the musical numbers does anything but illustrate the quality of the musical being produced—not very good.

The film is, however, in step with the times, since this is not a Broadway but an off-Broadway musical. Hence Jack Cole, again the choreographer, has scaled down the production numbers, but, amazingly within that small space, he gives full rein to his vulgarity.

The only decent song in the film is "My Heart Belongs to Daddy," by Cole Porter, originally sung by Mary Martin in *Leave It to Me* in 1938. Porter's lyric, full of double-entendre, must be sung with mock innocence if it is to have its comic effect. The song is not outside Marilyn Monroe's range as a performer. Her little girl's enjoyment of being sexy is not that far removed from Porter's little boy's glee in being suggestive. Jack Cole, however, stages the number for its lewdness and emphasizes the blowsy side of Monroe's personality. As she shakes and grinds all of her (in this film) considerable anatomy, the fun and sophistication of the song dies.

Marilyn Monroe struggles to be charming and kooky against the odds of the script, and Yves Montand almost collapses under his heroic struggles with the English language (it is his first American film), and he is totally done in by an abysmal slapstick pantomime. There seems to me no moments so awkwardly staged or so plodding in all of Cukor's films as those in the scenes in which Bing Crosby, Gene Kelly, and Milton Berle attempt to teach the billionaire their various arts. Everyone, actors and director included, seems embarrassed.

There is very little to redeem this film. Only the opening sequence, which traces the history of the billionaire's family through etchings, suggests Cukor's personality. (This, too, has its cringing moments, as when Montand's face is superimposed on the faces of people drawn by famous artists.) The color work is good, but the rest of the art direction is inferior. After Cukor's work on the Gordon-Kanin scripts, it is a shame to see him settle for such a pasteboard New York. Some of the shots of Greenwich Village suggest certain parts of London more than they do New York.

Cukor has spoken of how much he liked Monroe:
Her face moves—*it catches the light—it's genuinely photogenic. And she* thinks boldly. *She thinks as a dog thinks.* Au fond, *her mind is wonderfully unclouded—she doesn't censor her thoughts. She's like Elvis Presley, like all great performers—whenever she enters, it's an occasion.*[41]

It is unfortunate that star and director did not work together on a better property. Cukor was directing Monroe in *Something's Got To Give*, a remake of Leo McCarey's *My Favorite Wife*, when the actress died in 1962.

My Fair Lady (1964). Produced by Jack L. Warner for Warner Bros. Pictures, Inc. Script by Alan Jay Lerner, from the musical play by Lerner, adapted from *Pygmalion* by George Bernard Shaw. Music by Frederick Loewe. Lyrics by Alan Jay Lerner. Photographed by Harry Stradling. Edited by William Ziegler. Costumes and settings by Cecil Beaton. Choreography by Hermes Pan. With Rex Harrison (Henry Higgins), Audrey Hepburn (Eliza Doolittle), Stanley Holloway (Alfred Doolittle), Wilfrid Hyde-White (Colonel Pickering), Gladys Cooper (Mrs. Higgins), Jeremy Brett (Freddie), Theodore Bikel (Zoltan Karpathy), Mona Washbourne (Mrs. Pearce), Isobel Elsom (Mrs. Eynsford-Hill), Moyna MacGill (Mrs. Boxington), Baroness Rothschild (Princess of Transylvania), Henry Daniell (Prince of Transylvania).

One of the few books to deal with the collaborative effort of Hollywood superproduction in an informative way is *Cecil Beaton's "Fair Lady."*[42] It is no secret that Cukor and Beaton did not have the happiest relationship. Cukor has said, "I don't like Beaton. He was the only sour note in the whole picture."[43] Their mutual animosity runs through Beaton's book like a Wagnerian leitmotif. Cukor would have preferred Hoyningen-Huene, but Beaton, who had costumed the stage production, had been contracted for the film before the director was chosen.

In one of the earliest conferences on the film, Beaton reports: *When, at last, George thumbed through to the last page (of Beaton's costume sketches) he screwed up his face. "I didn't care for 'The Rain in Spain' costume you did for Julie Andrews. We must make Audrey look slightly—er—er—comic in that scene, as if Mrs. Pearce had been out and bought a dress from—who's your Pear and Does? Jack Robinson? She should look clean but not* chic*, and that's going to be awfully difficult because Audrey looks* chic *in anything. Also, at Ascot, she should seem somewhat—er—overpowered by her finery. She shouldn't be quite able to—er—carry it off. Try and devise a costume that will work dramatically to accentuate the comic content of the scene.*[44]

In another passage, Beaton tells how Alan Jay Lerner thought of the opening sequences of the film after looking at the costume sketches:

Alan saw the costumes and, at the sight of them, decided on a sudden switch for the beginning of the film. Instead of starting off with the poverty of Covent Garden, we would see the elegant Wagnerites leaving the Opera, running through the market in a sudden squall, then working up to a great entrance for rain-sodden Eliza.[45]

The reference to the Wagnerites implies that the collaborators were consciously trying to evoke the memory of Bernard Shaw for the film audiences, because Shaw was, of course, the first defender of Wagner in English musical circles. Similarly, the costumes for Mrs. Higgins were designed to reflect the taste of a "Fabian, a rather aesthetic intellectual" to emphasize that the character was based upon Shaw's own mother.

Beaton's book is an account of endless research, of poring over countless drawings of gowns by Lucille, Caillot, Cheruit, and Poiret for inspiration and authenticity. Beaton also passed along valuable research to other collaborators; for instance, he showed choreographer Hermes Pan drawings by Sem and Drian of the Forzane Slouch. Forzane was the last of the 1914 cocottes, and her walk, with her hips thrust forward as she dragged one foot behind, inspired the choreography for the "Ascot Gavotte."

All this research is admirable, but the question is, did it pay off? In the department of costumes, it did. They are elegant and lush, and yet comic when that is required (Eliza's costume for the Ascot meet is a particular triumph). The sets, however, are a failure, because they lack a unified approach. They range from the stylized realism of Covent Garden to the heavy literalness of Higgins's study, to the pasteboard, theatrical flimsiness of the ballroom, to the Art Nouveau salon of Mrs. Higgins, which has the appearance of a contemporary magazine illustration rather than that of a real living room. The art work is particularly unsuccessful in the Ascot Gavotte sequence. As on the stage, the set and costumes are entirely black and white, but the camera pulls back to show green grass under the singers' feet. This one new color destroys the artful stylization of this scene.

My Fair Lady was criticized for being a slavish and lifeless reproduction of the stage play when in fact, with the exception of the Ascot Gavotte sequence, very little of the film duplicates the original. In many ways the changes made in the film version are for the worse—the sets (done on the stage by Oliver Smith) are much lusher but not nearly so good; many of the songs have been re-thought for the screen, but they are not so effective. Some, such as "Get Me to the Church on Time," have been so prosaically edited that they lose the feeling of mounting exuberance. In "Just You Wait, 'Enry 'Iggins," Eliza's day-dreamed retributions are visualized so prosaically by Cukor that they totally kill the malicious glee of the song.

From its opening scenes, the staged *My Fair Lady* is rich, tasteful, and intelligent, and one feels comfortable within its values. It is not until "The Rain in Spain," how-ever, that the play really galvanizes the audience. This is the kind of moment, however, that rarely occurs on the screen, for it depends upon an electricity created by the interaction between audience and live performers. Though "The Rain in Spain" is still the highlight of the film ver-sion, it doesn't overwhelm the audience in the same way. Consequently the film does not gather momentum, and from beginning to end it never taps that vein of life that seems to lie just below the surface.

Another problem of the film is Rex Harrison's re-creation of his performance of Henry Higgins. Cukor has discussed this specific problem of actors:

Many times I have had the problem of working with an actor who was re-creating a stage role for the screen, going back to Freddie March in The Royal Family *as well as Rex Harrison, Judy Holliday, and Kate Hepburn. Well, they know the part very well. In fact, Rex said it was frightfully difficult because he has never played anything on screen which he had done on the stage. What you must do in that case is to give it a sense of improvisation. It's a whole new thing . . . you give a different performance. Naturally, they know the values, but they mustn't give a*

My Fair Lady: Audrey Hepburn, Rex Harrison
My Fair Lady: Rex Harrison, Audrey Hepburn, Wilfrid Hyde-White

stage performance. They must realize that everything is closer. You've got to give that sense that they have never done it before, which is the greatest strength of picture acting. Very often, when they've done it a certain way on the stage, you change it a tiny bit so that it comes out fresh because every performance on the screen must have that freshness. You can't play from point to point; and yet of course, they know where those points are. You can't wait for laughs and you can't build to the laughs, although in the back of their heads, they know the value of all these things. Judy Holliday was very funny because when she was rehearsing scenes she'd get a laugh from the stagehands. Then, we'd say, "All right, here we go," and she'd do it and there'd be these awful silences. It really threw her because she was used to getting those laughs. Rex was wonderful about that because in the lyrics and throughout the play, one never had the sense that he knew what was coming; he made it fresh. That was the trick—and it is a trick which intelligent actors are aware of.[46]

I'm afraid that I must disagree with Cukor. Harrison goes through his once-brilliant performance by rote. Stanley Holloway, also from the New York and London companies, should have been just as tired of his part of Alfred Doolittle, but he still manages to give the impression of being fresh and new. He is one of the few delights of the film.

The other major delight is Audrey Hepburn as Eliza. She beautifully catches the "Cinderella" quality of the role. She brings a true magic to the transformation scene when she appears on the balcony of Higgins' study in a gossamer Edwardian ball gown. It is true that Miss Hepburn does not really give herself to the early sequences of the guttersnipe Eliza: she plays at vulgarity; behind the façade peeps out the winking eye of a soignée actress. But then neither was Miss Andrews successful in those scenes. Indeed, there is a theatrical legend that claims the early Eliza Doolittle is unplayable, but Wendy Hiller in the film version of *Pygmalion* succeeds brilliantly. Beginning with the Ascot Gavotte scene, Miss Hepburn takes the role and finds a triumph in it. She has always been an actress assured at wearing a bittersweet heart on her sleeve—a quality befitting the transformed Eliza—but here she also exhibits an unexpected comedic talent with great dexterity of timing.

Miss Hepburn wanted to sing for herself and was promised she could do so, with perhaps some dubbing on the upper notes. She has a thinnish, far from secure voice, but one with great charm, as she had shown in *Funny Face*. However, the ubiquitous Marni Nixon supplied the colorless Jeanette MacDonald-ish soprano that rings from Miss Hepburn's lips. Frederick Loewe's music is not so sacrosanct that it needs this kind of hallowed operetta-ish respect. If Harrison could deliver his songs in an Americanized recitative, there is no reason why Hepburn shouldn't deliver hers in her own humanly vulnerable voice.

Bhowani Junction: Stewart Granger, Ava Gardner

Faraway Places
and Wide Open Spaces

In the first few years of the wide-screen processes, when no one was quite sure how to fill in all that empty space, one of the answers was to place a story inside a travelogue of some foreign locale. More than ever before Hollywood went on location. With the exception of *Edward, My Son,* Cukor had never shot outside of the United States. In 1955 he went to Pakistan to film *Bhowani Junction* (some of which was also shot in England). *Bhowani Junction* was also to give Cukor the chance to disprove the snub implied when Selznick fired him from *Gone with the Wind,* for it was a film that included lots of spectacle and action.

Bhowani Junction (1955). Produced by Pandro S. Berman for Metro-Goldwyn-Mayer. Script by Sonya Levein and Ivan Moffat, from the novel by John Masters. Photographed by Frederick Young. Color consultation by George Hoyningen-Huene. Edited by Frank Clarke and George Boemler. With Ava Gardner (Victoria Jones), Stewart Granger (Colonel Rodney Savage), Abraham Sofaer (Surabhai), Bill Travers (Patrick Taylor), Francis Matthews (Ranjit Kasel), Marne Maitland (Govindaswami), Peter Illing (Ghanshyam), Edward Chapman (Thomas Jones), Lionel Jeffries (Lieutenant Graham McDaniel), Freda Jackson (The Sedani).

Up to this point in Cukor's films, crowd scenes were limited to groups gathered at social functions—teas, weddings, dances, theater intermissions. The first few shots of *Bhowani Junction* present a new terrain: approaching head-on is a huge, lumbering train, pulling into an Indian station teeming with life. From the train descends half-caste Victoria Jones (Ava Gardner), wearing the uniform of a women's branch of the British Army. She is greeted by other British officers and, as the camera follows, they wend their way through the station. Though there is nothing innovatingly creative about the sequence, it is strikingly staged to catch a real sense of being part of a foreign crowd.

Bhowani Junction is a very handsome film. It intrigues the eye both with its superb sense of color and with some extremely artful composition. Cukor and his photographer, the gifted Frederick Young (who had previously shot *Edward, My Son* for Cukor and was later to do brilliant work on *Lawrence of Arabia*) have found ways to incorporate both perspective and intimacy into the flat, panoramic screen. There is one composition which is both visually striking and dramatically telling. Victoria returns to her parents' home. In the parlor she greets her English father, and then, moving down a dark hall, calls to her mother who appears from a doorway. Victoria embraces her Indian mother while the camera stays at a respectful distance. The editing and composition here succinctly state Victoria's dilemma of being torn between two different nationalities.

The film contains a number of spectacular scenes, including a train wreck and a chase at the film's end. These are well photographed and edited and are quite exciting. They would seem to belie Selznick's snub of Cukor as a "man of the theater," yet it is difficult to be absolutely certain. As we have seen, Cukor readily admits that many of the action sequences in *A Woman's Face* were really not his work. Although Cukor undoubtedly supervised and approved them, probably the spectacular sequences in *Bhowani Junction* were done by a special-effects unit or by an assistant director, greatly aided by the editor.

Bhowani Junction was based on a best-selling novel by John Masters which dealt with the fate of Anglo-Indians just prior to and immediately following India's liberation from Great Britain. Purportedly a serious novel, it really loses the political realities it strives to depict in the fic-

Bhowani Junction: Ava Gardner

tional romance of Victoria and her British colonel, Rodney Savage. In reshaping the novel as a screenplay, the political aspects were further diluted so that the conventional love story comes all the more to the front.

The flaw, however, is compensated for not only by the attractiveness of the *mise en scène* but also by the extraordinary presence of Ava Gardner in the role of Victoria. Cukor has said that he believes Miss Gardner has handicapped herself by underrating her skills as an actress. One cannot honestly bring to bear conventional criteria in judging Miss Gardner's performance. Her emotional range and technique are adequate to meet the limited demands of this and most of her other roles. (Here she is unnecessarily handicapped by dialogue that tries for the intonation and phraseology of Indian English.) What one responds to is the intense sensuality of her presence.

Cukor filmed two sequences for *Bhowani Junction* which as described would seem to have been the most erotic of all his work. One showed a love scene between Ava Gardner and Bill Travers, which the director remembers as being very similar to the famous orgasm sequence in Louis Malle's *The Lovers* (1958); the other is one in which Miss Gardner, after taking a shower, washes out her mouth with whiskey poured in her lover's tooth glass. These scenes were censored in 1955. It was the sensual side of *Bhowani Junction*, rather than the spectacle, which really seemed to intrigue Cukor and challenged him to think of methods to depict physical intimacy in an adult and tasteful way.

Although Cukor is noted for his ability to enhance the performances given by his leading ladies, he rarely does so by emphasizing their sexual allure. Until his meeting with Miss Gardner, there are no erotically oriented performances in his films (though there is an occasional erotic moment growing out of the character, as is the case with Garbo in *Camille*). Cukor is interested in his leading ladies and the characters they play as female human beings rather than as sex objects. His handling of those female stars who were out-and-out sex symbols tends to personalize their sexuality by placing it within a comic perspective—Jean Harlow is brassy and vulgarly funny; Sophia Loren is amused; Marilyn Monroe is kittenish and perky. To Miss Gardner, however, Cukor responds with great sensuality. The camera lingers over her with loving attention and finds settings and compositions to enhance her beauty.

Wild Is the Wind (1957). Produced by Hal B. Wallis for Paramount Pictures Corp. Script by Arnold Schulman, from a story by Vittorio Nino Novarese. Photographed by Charles Lang, Jr. and Lloyd Grigges. Edited by Warren Low. With Anna Magnani (Gioia), Anthony Quinn (Gino), Anthony Franciosa (Bene), Lili Valenty (Teresa), Joseph Calleia (Alberto), Dolores Hart (Angie), Highland Dale.

This story of passion among Italian sheep farmers in Nevada does not seem to be the kind of material that would greatly appeal to Cukor, and neither do the screenwriter or most of the cast appear to be his likeliest group of collaborators. *Wild Is the Wind* is an extremely close variant of Sidney Howard's 1924 play, *They Knew What They Wanted* (which later became the musical *The Most Happy Fella*). In fact, it is in outline *exactly* the same story, with a different setting, and slight differences among the character relationships. The play, with its warm human story and its serio-comic plot, might well have appealed to Cukor, and he perhaps felt he could achieve the same ends with this rather pale imitation.

Arnold Schulman's script is heavy-handed. There is some embarrassingly facile symbolism concerning some wild horses. Magnani wants them to run free, but Quinn wants to shoot them. Finally Quinn tames one as a present for Magnani, but she doesn't want it domesticated; wild things should be left wild like the wind.

Probably what appealed to Cukor most about this production was the chance to work with the great Anna Magnani. Though the role is too similar to characters that the actress had already played for her to have fresh impact, Magnani is still marvelous in all the old ways. Much of her method of acting—the large hand gestures, the sudden bursts of anger or enthusiasm, her ability to register dawning disbelief or awareness, her extremely natural movement and line-reading—begin here to appear like mannerisms. Still she sweeps one away with the sheer force of her naked emotionalism.

Technically, *Wild Is the Wind* is not good, with the exception of some imaginative framing of the VistaVision screen. The outdoor action scenes look as if they had been shot by a second-unit company, and they are jarringly matched with close-ups of the principal actors standing against suspiciously studio-looking backgrounds. For whatever reason these sequences are not nearly so good as those in *Bhowani Junction*.

Heller in Pink Tights (1959). Produced by Carlo Ponti and Marcello Girosi for Paramount Pictures Corp. Script by Dudley Nichols and Walter Bernstein from the novel, *Heller with a Gun*, by Louis L'Amour. Photographed by Howard Lipstein. Color consultation by George Hoyning-en-Huene. Edited by Howard Smith. With Sophia Loren (Angele Rossini), Anthony Quinn (Tom Healy), Margaret O'Brien (Dall Southby), Steve Forrest (Mabry), Eileen Heckart (Lorna Hathaway), Edmund Lowe (Manfred "Doc" Montague), Ramon Novarro (DeLeon), Frank Cordell (Theodore).

Wild Is the Wind: Anthony Franciosa, Anna Magnani, Anthony Quinn
Heller in Pink Tights: Sophia Loren, Anthony Quinn

Heller in Pink Tights is Cukor's only attempt at a Western, but it is a very personal Western since it involves a traveling theatrical troupe in the saloon days of the West. Much of it is extremely pleasant, particularly those sequences that deal with the performances which the troupe gives of *Mazeppa* and Offenbach's *La Belle Hélène*. *Heller in Pink Tights* is visually one of Cukor's most handsome films—the sets, costumes, and color are striking. Cukor credits the charm of the costumes to Hoyning-en-Huene:

George went down into the basement of the studio, to the wardrobe storage place where nobody ever goes, and he came back with old costumes of the crusades, the Revolution . . . all sorts of incorrect things falling apart and he put them all together. It was so real on the screen, all the actors in the far West with this incredible mélange.[47]

A great deal of research was done on this production. Cukor remembers:

We saw pictures of Indians and I don't think Indians had ever looked that way because these were photographs of real Indians exactly the way they were. And then we saw pictures of what the men in the West looked like. We reproduced that Western dress; I'd never done a Western and I loved doing it.[48]

Despite its visual beauty, the film is curiously flat. There are a lot of action sequences, and though they are done more carefully than the ones in *Wild Is the Wind,* they aren't very exciting. Nor is the screenplay, beyond its initial premise, that intriguing. Sophia Loren, decked out in a blonde wig, seems rather muted as she does in most of her American films, but she is charming. The rest of the cast, with the exception of Margaret O'Brien and Eileen Heckart who have a few amusing moments as a stage mother-and-daughter team, adds to the film's somewhat listless impression.

Evidently, Cukor does not approve of the final edited version of this film, so perhaps not so much has been made of the footage as could have been. It is a film whose parts are much better than the whole. This picture was a great deal more successful in France than it was in America, and Cukor feels that it may have influenced Louis Malle's *Viva Maria!* which concerns two showgirls in the wilds of South America.

Justine (1969). Produced by Pandro S. Berman for Twentieth Century-Fox Film Corp. Script by Lawrence B. Marcus, from *The Alexandria Quartet* by Lawrence Durrell. Photographed by Leon Shamroy. Edited by Rita Rowland. With Anouk Aimée (Justine), Dirk Bogarde (Pursewarden), Robert Forster (Narouz), Anna Karina (Melissa), Philippe Noiret (Pombal), Michael York (Darley), John Vernon (Nessim), Jack Albertson (Cohen), Cliff Gorman (Toto), Michael Constantine (Memlik Pasha), Marcel Dalio (French Consul General), Michael Dunn (Mnemijian), Barry Morse (Maskelyne), Severn Darden (Balthazar).

Justine was one of the most trouble-ridden productions of recent years. Originally Twentieth Century-Fox assigned producer Walter Wanger and writer-director Joseph L. Mankiewicz to bring *Justine* to the screen. The company had a falling out with producer and director over *Cleopatra* and took the property away from them. For the next few years, Fox went through a number of screenwriters who tried to solve the problem of adapting the four convoluted novels which comprise Lawrence Durrell's *The Alexandria Quartet* into a single feature-length film. Finally Lawrence Marcus (whose credentials hardly guaranteed that he would be the man for the job) got what Fox considered a workable screenplay, and they hired director Joseph Strick who had just had a success with his version of James Joyce's *Ulysses*. The company began shooting in Tunis (the story was set in Egypt). Within a few weeks Strick was fired, and Cukor replaced him.

Since Cukor did not have any say over the screenplay or the casting of the film, and since these two elements so often give Cukor films their character, *Justine* can be considered a film of marginal importance to his career. Cukor has discussed his feelings about working under these conditions:

As far as the Larry Marcus script is concerned I think it's excellent, although I think we might have wanted the film to be about an hour longer. I think all those interesting characters could easily have stood more time on film. But I still feel I have achieved something with the time allotted. . . . I must say I don't and didn't like the idea of working with a group of actors that I hadn't taken any part in selecting. It's not that they were bad or anything—in fact Dirk Bogarde was marvelous. But Anouk was a bit of a problem. In certain scenes she was simply wonderful—the whole section with the mirrors—all those different views—holding the cigarette in a certain way that introduced a whole vulgar, hard quality to Justine that really is a part of the character. And Anna Karina, now, she too had some problems readjusting to coming to Hollywood after the Tunis shooting. One day on the set she came running up to me, like a child, weeping that her hair was completely wrong for the scene or she didn't want to look like that or something. I was rather firm. One just can't allow this kind of behavior to continue or be indulged if any work is going to take place. So I screamed a little and said you had better stop this. I mean, making a film is not like discussing your private life with someone. I would never do that. Work is work and being neurotic is for close friends. Professionalism is not just an attitude that one develops—it has to be in some way accepting one's role in the work at hand. That's why even with a script that I had no part in developing it was essential to forget myself and get down to making the film.[49]

Perhaps no one could turn Durrell's books into a workable screenplay of average length, but certainly Marcus hasn't. The script is utter confusion even to someone who has read all the books. With the exceptions of Anouk Aimée, Anna Karina, and Dirk Bogarde, the film is entirely miscast. Against these odds Cukor fails to re-create the author's world of fetid sensuality, political intrigue, and moral fatigue. Nor does he capture the sense of magic inherent in the constantly shifting identities and relationships of the characters. Durrell's sensibility goes against the grain of Cukor's. The writer is flamboyant, purple-prosed, in love with the sound of words, and to bring his world to life on film one needs a director with a true sensual response to the plasticity of the medium. It needs a bit of the kind of showing off that Cukor's approach prevents.

The Chapman Report: Claire Bloom, Glynis Johns

Odds and Ends

The following minor films were made during various periods but do not fit into the main phases of Cukor's career.

Zaza (1938). Produced by Albert Lewin for Paramount Pictures. Script by Zoë Akins, from the play by Pierre Breton and Charles Simon. Photographed by Charles Lang. Songs by Al Hoffman and Frank Loesser. Edited by Edward Dmytryk. With Claudette Colbert (Zaza), Herbert Marshall (Dufresne), Bert Lahr (Cascart), Helen Westley (Anais), Constance Collier (Nathalie), Genevieve Tobin (Florianne), Walter Catlett (Malardot), Rex O'Malley (Bussey), Ann Todd (Toto).

From the credits, *Zaza* seems like a promising Cukor film. The script writer and some members of the cast are past collaborators in successful films, and there are a number of his personal friends involved in the project. Though he had never worked before with Claudette Colbert or Herbert Marshall, they seem actors who would be congenial to his personality. The script is based on a very famous play in which Mrs. Leslie Carter had had a great success at the turn of the century. It later was turned into an opera by Leoncavallo, and with Geraldine Farrar in the lead it was a great popular favorite at the Metropolitan Opera in New York during the 1920s.

Unfortunately, the promise is not fulfilled. The plot concerns adultery—Zaza is a cabaret performer who becomes involved with a married man—and the script could not be made acceptable to the Hays Office without removing from it all rhyme and reason. Consequently, the film is extremely flat. Cukor also feels that Claudette Colbert was miscast in the part of Zaza—that she is, on the one hand, too wholesome and, on the other, too sophisticated to play the part of a music-hall strumpet.

Also, this film might have been better were there more glimpses of backstage life and more cabaret numbers included to compensate for the flimsy material. The numbers that are included do not have strong musical values, but they are the liveliest part of the show. One wishes, too, that Cukor had made more use of the great Bert Lahr, who is muted throughout the film.

Resistance and Ohm's Law (1944). A documentary concerning the 18th-century German physicist, George Ohm, directed for the United States Signal Corps.

A Life of Her Own (1950). Produced by Voldemar Vetlunguin for Metro-Goldwyn-Mayer. Script by Isabel Lennart. Photographed by George Folsey. Edited by George White. With Lana Turner (Lily James), Ray Milland (Steve Harleigh), Tom Ewell (Tom Carraway), Ann Dvorak (Mary Ashlon), Barry Sullivan (Lee Garance), Margaret Phillips (Nora Harleigh), Jean Hagen (Maggie Collier).

George Cukor remembers very little about *A Life of Her Own,* but what he remembers is exact:
All I can remember about that one is that I hated it. It was an awful story. When we went to the first story conference, I couldn't believe my ears. It was terrible. At the beginning she was supposed to kill herself, and then they wouldn't even let her do that.[50]

This is a film without much interest, except for a flashy performance by Ann Dvorak as a drunken has-been model. It's made palatable by the plush MGM production values. Here Cukor's reputation as a woman's director meets head on with the talents of Lana Turner. She wins.

The Model and the Marriage Broker (1951). Produced by Charles Brackett for Twentieth Century-Fox Film Corp. Script by Charles Brackett, Walter Reisch, and Richard Breen. Photographed by Robert Simpson. Edited by Robert

Simpson. With Jeanne Crain (Kitty Bennett), Scott Brady (Walt Hornbeck), Thelma Ritter (Mae Swazey), Zero Mostel (Mr. Wisted), Michael O'Shea (Doberman), Helen Ford (Emmy Swazey), Frank Fontaine (Johann-son), Dennie Moore (Mrs. Gingrass), John Alexander (Mr. Perry), Jay C. Flippen (Dan Chancellor), Nancy Kulp (Hazel), Bunny Bishop (Alice), Maude Prickett (Delia).

The Model and the Marriage Broker was made during the period when Cukor was working mainly with scripts by Ruth Gordon and Garson Kanin. This script was written by Charles Brackett, Walter Reisch, and Richard Breen, and it has the New York setting, the colorful supporting roles, and the genial, rather folksy humor that characterize many of the Kanins' best scripts.

It is really quite a pleasant film. The script has a bad dramatic flaw in that the two young leads (Jeanne Crain and Scott Brady) get lost in the film, and their story is developed only in the most cursory way. Yet the film draws much of its strength from pushing the youngsters to the background and emphasizing the character roles, all beautifully played by some of the most familiar faces and least familiar names in the business. Thelma Ritter is unwisely at the center of a picture. Miss Ritter has a very definite character—that of a wisecracking, savvy dame who calls us up short by exposing that heart of gold. She does her bit better than any one else, and she is adorable when she is on the periphery of a film. Though Miss Ritter never mugs or overplays, one gets tired of her, simply because her personality isn't varied enough to carry the whole weight of a film.

Song Without End (1960). Produced by William Goetz for Columbia Pictures Corp. Directed by Charles Vidor. Script by Oscar Millard. Photographed by James Wong

Howe. Edited by William A. Lyon. With Dirk Bogarde (Franz Liszt), Capucine (Princess Caroline Sayn-Wittengenstein), Ivan Desny (Prince Nicholas Sayn-Wittengenstein), Martita Hunt (Grand Duchess of Weimar), Marcel Dalio (Chelard).

After three weeks of shooting on this film, director Charles Vidor died; Cukor succeeded him but asked that Vidor receive sole credit. This is at most a marginal film in Cukor's career, and it is doubtful he would have initiated it or, having done so, approved this script.

The Chapman Report (1963). Produced by Richard D. Zanuck for Warner Bros. Pictures, Inc. Screenplay by Wyatt Cooper and Don M. Mankiewicz, from an adaptation by Gene Allen and Grant Stuart of Irving Wallace's novel. Photographed by Harold Lipstein. Edited by Robert Simpson. With Efrem Zimbalist, Jr. (Paul Radford), Shelley Winters (Sarah Garnell), Jane Fonda (Kathleen Barclay), Claire Bloom (Naomi Shields), Glynis Johns (Teresa Harnish), Ray Danton (Fred Linden), Ty Hardin (Ed Kraski), Andre Duggan (Dr. George Chapman), John Dehner (Geoffrey Harnish), Harold J. Stone (Frank Garnell), Corey Allen (Wash Dillon), Cloris Leachman (Miss Selby), Henry Daniell (Dr. Jonas), Hope Cameron (Ruth Linden).

What happened to *The Chapman Report* before it reached the screen illustrates the changes and problems that can beset a property during gestation. In the early 1960s, Cukor owed a commitment to Twentieth Century-Fox, and the company was threatening to sue if he did not fulfill it. Cukor read Irving Wallace's best-selling novel, *The Chapman Report,* which Fox owned, and though he found it lurid, he was also amused by it and thought he could make a film from it that would be tasteful.

The Model and the Marriage Broker:
Scott Brady, Jeanne Crain, Thelma Ritter
The Chapman Report: Claire Bloom

Wallace's novel concerns six women who agree to be questioned in a sex survey à la Kinsey. It also deals with the investigators, only one of whom is beyond reproach. The characters are schematically conceived as a cross section of sexual malaise, and the sex scenes are rather tawdry though never graphic. What is objectionable about the novel (and most of this is removed in the finished film) is the somewhat hysterical mudslinging concerning the private motivations and morals of the survey team. Also questionable is Wallace's philistine point of view that sexual statistics are worthless because they omit the quotient of love. The finished film also supports this position. The only woman who is helped by the survey is the one whom an investigator, dropping his scientific anonymity, takes lovingly to bed.

Fox assigned Ron Alexander to fashion a screenplay.[51] He eliminated all the sympathetic characters, plugged away at the exposé of the investigators' private conduct, and made the sensational scenes even more sensational. Almost nothing of this screenplay was used, possibly because Cukor felt that *this* he couldn't film in good taste.

The screenplay that Cukor finally used was based on an adaptation by Gene Allen, a frequent collaborator of Cukor's. (Allen did the art direction on most of the director's color films, including *The Chapman Report*.) Undoubtedly, this screenplay was geared to Cukor's specifications. It eliminates the psychopathic murderer, retains the nymphomaniacal wife but excises her husband, and reduces Dr. Chapman to a minor, morally unquestionable character. In effect, it expunges much of the sensational, melodramatic twists of the plot. Also, to keep the script at a workable length, the writers have eliminated two of the women who had large roles in the novel.

By 1962, Fox was having a mammoth headache over the spiraling costs of *Cleopatra*. The company's continued existence was threatened as were the jobs of the higher echelons of personnel. Late in the same year, former president Darryl F. Zanuck returned to power. He immediately shut down all production of films not already shooting and threw out all properties bought by the previous regime, among them *The Chapman Report*. Zanuck decided to produce this film through his own independent producing unit. He established his son, Richard D. Zanuck, as nominal head of production and arranged for the film to be released by Warner's.

The shooting period evidently went smoothly. The trouble began after the first preview. Cukor remembers: *After the preview I made some minor suggestions about recutting, just re-working it a little. Then . . . we shipped the print over to Zanuck [who was in Europe making* The Longest Day]. *He, then, as usual, cut the damned thing, completely re-cut it so that it no longer made any sense at all. He emasculated it. . . . He just cut everything every sort of mad way, that's all . . . Warner's were appalled at what he had done . . . Warner's restored certain things, . . . and while they were doing this I said to them: "You know, if you cut out the high-minded parts of this thing the censors will jump down your throats because of the book's bad reputation."*[52]

The film was never restored the way Cukor wanted it, and the result was as the director had predicted: the censors insisted on cutting it further.

Practically all the critics jumped on the film, quite unfairly, because, even in its emasculated release version, it is a diverting film, filled with small sillinesses, to be sure, but never offensive. It is highly glossed and brilliantly hued, like the wealthy California households it depicts. Cukor has managed to make a silk purse out of a sow's ear, and in the bargain, filled it with a number of quite interesting performances.

By far the best performance in the film is Claire Bloom
as the nymphomaniac, Naomi Shields. Cukor has said
that he cast Miss Bloom in the role because he wanted
an actress who projected "class" in order to counteract
the sluttish side of the character. His choice of Miss
Bloom was particularly happy because she is an actress
who is most interesting when she is cast against her cool,
ladylike image. Her portrayal of Naomi is striking because
the actress never stoops to vamping the role in any obviously sexy way. Miss Bloom makes inherent in each of
Naomi's indiscretions—an attempted seduction of a delivery boy, a gang rape caused in part by her own
provocation—the character's own judgment of her actions.
The keynote of Miss Bloom's performance is that of icy,
unrelenting, inner-directed fury at what she cannot help
herself from doing. It is a harrowing performance, and
one of the best in all of Cukor's films.

Comic relief is supplied by Glynis Johns as the chirpy,
aesthetically oriented, happily mated Teresa Harnish. Initially quite winning, Miss Johns's performance eventually
becomes terribly silly because she plays the part on the
same, one note as it is written. Since this part was the
one least affected by the post-shooting cutting, the role
gains an importance it ought not to have.

The major character in the film was to have been
Kathleen Barclay, the frigid woman. According to Cukor,
this part was badly cut, and in the final film she has no
more importance than do the other women. It is not a
well-written part, with more than its share of silly moments and lines, but Jane Fonda, in her third film role,
manages to play it with more truth than is really in the
writing. The immaturity of her technique is evident in a
certain hesitancy about her playing and in the fact that
she is not able to ride over the rough spots in the script.
Still, she has an attractive and surprisingly flexible voice

and a sure ear for vocal inflection and coloration. Her neurotic outbursts are sudden, piercing, and emotionally well supported.

Shelley Winters gives the only weak performance in the film. As Sarah Garnell, the adulterous wife in love with a handsome but weak ladies' man, Miss Winters realizes all the potential flaws hinted at in her performance in *A Double Life*. The actress uses every vocal trick to emphasize the pathetic vulnerability of the character. She plays with a cheap and obvious emotional identification with her character which certain Method actors by the 1960s were using to signal to their audiences that they were being "honest." It is a slovenly and tawdry performance, the only element in the film which remains staunchly loyal to the level of Wallace's novel.

The one new note in Cukor's films in the last fifteen years has been a flirtation with erotic or sensual subject matter. As I have said, I think this was the director's primary interest in *Bhowani Junction* and probably also in *The Chapman Report*. Despite the cutting, *The Chapman Report* does show the director's handling of such material: Clare Bloom attempts to seduce a delivery boy. Miss Bloom is nude underneath a filmy peignoir, and the scene is shot with a filtered, rather seamy lighting. The camera adopts Miss Bloom's viewpoint because it is she who is the aggressor; it takes fleeting, provocative glances at the man's body. There is very little bodily contact in the scene and no real nudity. What Cukor is attempting is to create a sexual tension between the couple that will so permeate the scene that it will become almost tangible to the audience. With the greatest taste, with tact even, he succeeds.

Notes

1. From a series of unpublished interviews with George Cukor by Robert Hughes, conducted early 1967.
2. Twenty-three plays, eleven novels—*Camille* is here included in the novels, for that was its original form.
3. Marguerite Courtney, *Laurette* (New York: Atheneum, 1955), p. 297.
4. *Ibid.*
5. *Ibid.*
6. *Ibid.,* p. 313.
7. *Ibid.*, p. 314.
8. Hughes interviews with Cukor.
9. It was not quite his last. In 1956 he was engaged to direct Enid Bagnold's *The Chalk Garden.* It was an unhappy experience, involving differences of opinion with the various artistic elements. Cukor withdrew before the play's (successful) New York opening. He has said that the experience left him with no desire to work on the stage again.
10. No two sources agree on dating films. Europeans date from the year of production; Americans date from first release, which generally means the first appearance of the film in any part of the country. I have tried to find the initial release date in the United States, but I am sure I have not always been successful. There is a particular problem when a film borders on the end of a year: for instance, an MGM press release on *Keeper of the Flame* is dated December 1942, but the film opened in New York March 1943 —this does not mean that it did not open elsewhere prior to its New York premiere. Hence my decision as to where to place a film has been in some cases arbitrary.
11. Hughes interviews with Cukor.
12. Gene Ringgold, "Constance Bennett," *Films in Review* (New York), October 1965.

13. Hughes interviews with Cukor.
14. Alistair Cooke, "The Filming of 'Little Women,' " *The Listener* (London), October 15, 1933.
15. Much of this information on *Gone with the Wind* is drawn from Ronald Bryden's article, "Epic," *The Observer* (London), January 7, 1968. Despite small inaccuracies, this appears to be the most carefully researched and unbiased report yet written about the making of this important film. There remain, however, various reports of how long Cukor worked on the actual shooting; figures vary from ten days to three weeks.
16. *Ibid.*
17. Kenneth Tynan, "The Genius and the Girls: George Cukor," *Holiday* (New York), February 1961, p. 99. Reprinted as "George Cukor and the Girls," *Tynan Right and Left* (New York: Atheneum, 1961). This seems not only an ungracious remark but also transparently false. Considering the number of films Cukor made for Selznick and the fact that *Gone with the Wind* had been in the planning stages for three years, it seems rather late in the day for the producer to reach this conclusion.
18. Bryden, "Epic."
19. Hughes interviews with Cukor.
20. *Ibid.* Katharine Hepburn was present during some of the interviews.
21. Cukor once planned to film Barrie's play with Audrey Hepburn in the lead.
22. Hughes interviews with Cukor.
23. Miss Shearer received vocal coaching for this role from Constance Collier.
24. Hughes interviews with Cukor.
25. In an interview with Richard Overstreet (*Film Culture* [New York], Fall 1964, p. 16) Cukor said

of Garbo, "You have to give her her head—let her do what she feels. If you remember in *Camille* when the father comes in to tell her to leave his son, she falls to the ground and puts her hand on the table. That's a very original thing to do. One must let her do these things, and they happen marvelously."

26. Hughes interviews with Cukor.

27. "Habina and Sorel," *The New Republic* (New York), January 5, 1927, p. 190. Reprinted in *Immortal Shadows* (New York: Charles Scribner's Sons, 1947).

28. Joan Crawford with Jane Kesner Ardmore, *A Portrait of Joan* (Garden City, New York: Doubleday, 1962), pp. 126–27.

29. Hughes interviews with Cukor.

30. Quoted by Kathleen Tynan, "Great Kate," *Vogue* (New York), April 15, 1969, p. 88.

31. In New York it was known as *Angel Street* and opened in 1941 with Judith Evelyn and Vincent Price in the leads; it ran for 1,295 performances. Also in 1941 it was filmed in England by Thorold Dickinson under its original title, though when it was released in America many years later it was called *Angel Street*. When MGM made their version of the play, they bought and suppressed the Dickinson film.

32. James Agee, "Film," *The Nation* (New York), January 6, 1945. Reprinted in *Agee on Film: Reviews and Comments by James Agee* (New York: Beacon Press, 1958).

33. Hughes interviews with Cukor.

34. *Ibid.*

35. *Ibid.*

36. In "The Private Kate," *McCall's* (New York, February 1970, p. 60, Garson Kanin recalls that Tracy often quoted his idol, George M. Cohan, "What ever you do, kid, always serve it with a little dressing."

37. Ruth Gordon's delightful article, "Those Years After *Years Ago,"* published 1947, *The New York Times,* reprinted in *The Passionate Playgoer,* ed. George Oppenheimer (New York: Viking, 1958), tells what happened to her between the time she left her family home and was hired for her first part in Maude Adams's 1915 revival of *Peter Pan* (part of this time was spent working as an extra in films). This article has a great deal more of the flavor of becoming an actress than does her play.
38. Overstreet interview with Cukor, p. 3.
39. *Ibid.,* p. 7.
40. Cole Porter was ill at the time he was composing this music, and he admitted the songs were poor. See his biography by George Eells, *The Life that Late He Lead* (New York: G. P. Putnam's Sons, 1967), p. 307.
41. *Tynan Right and Left,* p. 271.
42. *Cecil Beaton's Fair Lady* (New York: Holt, Rinehart and Winston, 1964).
43. Overstreet interview with Cukor, p. 11. Beaton and Cukor had collaborated once before, on the stage production of *The Chalk Garden.* It seems that one of the reasons Cukor withdrew from the production was his antipathy toward Beaton.
44. *Cecil Beaton's Fair Lady*, p. 30.
45. *Ibid.*, p. 47.
46. Hughes interviews with Cukor.
47. Overstreet interview with Cukor, p. 10.
48. Hughes interviews with Cukor.
49. Aubrey Tarbox interview with Cukor, *Inter/view* (New York), September 1969.
50. Overstreet interview with Cukor, p. 15.
51. This script, dated May 1, 1961, is in the Film Archives of The Museum of Modern Art, New York.
52. Overstreet interview with Cukor, pp. 1–2.

On the set of *My Fair Lady*